Temptations of a Superpower

■ ■ ■

The Joanna Jackson Goldman Memorial Lecture
on American Civilization and Government

Temptations of a Superpower

. . .

Ronald Steel

Harvard University Press

Cambridge, Massachusetts
London, England
1995

E
840
. S 725
1995

LIBRARY OF CONGRESS CATALOGING-IN-PUBLICATION DATA

Steel, Ronald.
Temptations of a superpower / Ronald Steel.
p.   cm. — (The Joanna Jackson Goldman memorial lecture on
American civilization and government)
Includes bibliographical references.
ISBN 0-674-87340-8 (acid-free paper)
1. United States—Foreign relations—1989-   2. Post-communism.
I. Title.   II. Series.
E840.S725   1995
327.73—dc20   94-40791
CIP

for Kathy

Acknowledgments

■ ■ ■

This book is based on a presentation delivered at the Library of Congress in Washington, D.C., in November 1993. It inaugurated the annual lectureship named after Joanna Jackson Goldman. This series is designed to stimulate discussion of issues in American civilization and government. It was made possible by a gift from the estate of the late historian Eric F. Goldman, and was begun in honor of his late wife, Joanna.

I am gratified at having been chosen by the Library, acting in consultation with advisors from the Goldman estate, particularly Daniel J. Kevles and Aida Donald. Their encouragement persuaded me to present the lecture and to expand it considerably into the modest book that it has become. The directors of the Library provided both a distinguished setting and a festive atmosphere for the delivery of this lecture.

Although my friends share no blame for my judgments or errors, I am grateful to Sidney Blumenthal, Thomas L. Hughes, Tamar Jacoby and Benjamin C. Schwarz for their immensely helpful comments on the manuscript.

Contents

■ ■ ■

Temptations of a Superpower

■ ■ ■

Introduction

During the Cold War we had a vocation; now we have none. Once we had a powerful enemy; now it is gone. Once we had obedient allies; now we have trade rivals. Once we used to know how to define our place in the world and what our interests were; now we have no idea. Once we fretted about what critics called our arrogance of power. Now we wonder whether we are too timid and cautious.

The world we knew has collapsed around us. Nations that were once meek and disciplined are now violent and chaotic. Peoples who once lived together with apparent contentment now go for each other's throats. Until the Cold War was over we did not appreciate that the conflict, for all its inequities and dangers, imposed a kind of order on the world. Now even that is gone.

Of course there is our victory. But what do we do with it? Our rival collapsed so suddenly and ignominiously, looking more like a deflated blowfish than a whale. This left us confused and even a bit bereft. We had arrived at the arena garbed like a gladiator, while our opponent shuffled in wearing rags and shaking a paper cup.

Yes, the other side lost. But did we win? And if so, was it because of our superior strength and values? Or did we merely have deeper pockets than our foe? And what does it mean to win? What do we do with our victory?

Our politicians trumpet that we are the last remaining superpower. Or at least they used to, before the phrase started giving off a hollow ring. Superpowers, after all, are supposed to be superpowerful: to crack heads, lock up lawbreakers, and strike fear into the hearts of the wicked.

But what does it mean to be a superpower these days? Who wants to pay the bills? During the Gulf war we learned that our government didn't. What is the point of being a superpower if there is only one of them?

The whole meaning of the superpower tango is that it is a duet. Superpowers "contain," challenge, intimidate, and even threaten to fight one another. They speak the same language and respond to the same buttons when pushed. They assemble alliances, rattle sabers, and periodically meet at "summits" to keep things from getting out of hand.

But how does a superpower bring democracy to Haiti or resolve the ethnic quarrels of Bosnia? How does it frighten terrorists it cannot even find? How does it punish trading partners, like China, for domestic abuse when it wants to keep two-way trade flowing? How does it intimidate warlords from Pale to Mogadishu who know that they will still be around long after the cop on the beat has decided that it is time to go home?

The Cold War, by contrast, was easy to figure out. We signed up allies by the dozens, propped up friendly tyrants, bought off greedy neutrals, fought wars in remote and unlikely places for abstract causes, and patrolled the frontiers of what we staked out as the "free world." Every arena was critical, every problem, by definition, a crisis.

But the old rules have been turned upside down. Instead of "containing" the Russians, we now subsidize them. The Third World, where we fought and financed wars we considered crucial, is now a political sinkhole. And the nations we used to consider Cold War allies are now merely rapacious trading partners.

The Cold War, despite its ideological overlay, was a classic conflict among states. We and the Soviets vied for king of the mountain. Today the most violent disputes lie outside the state system: in ethnic, religious, and tribal feuds. Many of these—like the wars in the Balkans, the Caucasus, and Central Africa—date back long before the Cold War, and even before this century.

Do we have any obligations to these troubled lands? Does it matter whether they are undemocratic, feel insecure, or fall into disarray? Around the world we have a string of "allies" that we nurture at considerable cost.

What sense do Cold War allies make without a Cold War?

The superpower syndrome declares that the United States must stand guard as global gendarme. When the Soviet Union was strong, our job was to "contain" it. Has that job now been completed? Not at all, some say. The world is still a messy and disorderly place. Someone has to keep order. Since we are a superpower, our strategists tell us, that is our job. There is no rest for the righteous. That is the meaning of the otherwise perplexing statement by Richard Nixon, who declared in his final book that "because we are the last remaining superpower, no crisis is irrelevant to our interests."[1]

A few years ago such a statement seemed to embody an obvious truth. But does it make any sense today? Why is no crisis irrelevant? Did Nixon, an enthusiastic Cold War game player, get his aphorism backwards? Could it be that because there is no other superpower, and indeed no powerful enemies, a good many crises are, in fact, irrelevant?

Such a notion is hard for foreign policy professionals to deal with. For three generations they have made a career of running the world. They operated on the belief that in the contest with Soviet communism every place was a "crisis area." But that contest is over. Today the competition has moved elsewhere: to the industrial megalith of Japan, to the nimble trading states of Southeast Asia, to the emerging colossus of China, and to the giant emporium of a uniting Europe.

These countries do not want to bury capitalism. On the contrary, they are determined to do it better than we do. While we struggle with our role of superpower, they concentrate on productivity, market penetration, wealth, and innovation: the kind of power that matters most in today's world. In this competition we are—with our chronic deficits, weak currency, massive borrowing, and immense debt—a very strange kind of superpower.

In one sense we recognize this. Yet we are still hobbled by our Cold War ways of looking at the world, and by the temptations to intervene everywhere that go along with the self-definition of "superpower." Our policymakers continue to invoke our "vital national interest" in "world order," and they stake out a "security environment" of global dimensions.

But as they spin these scenarios, what world are they living in? Do we, who are expected to support them, know what they are talking about? Indeed, do they?

1
...

An Ambiguous Victory

History plays strange jokes on nations, as it does on people. We are now living the curse of those who get what they ask for. Only a few years ago we yearned for the disappearance of what Ronald Reagan called the "evil empire" and for victory in the Cold War. We got our wish. The Soviet Union is no more, communism is discredited, and free market capitalism is trumpeted in the corridors of the Kremlin.

By the standards of the Cold War we should be in a triumphant mood. With the demise of the Soviet Union, the United States stands in magnificent splendor as the world's only remaining superpower. Our fleets and air squadrons roam the world unimpeded by any rival force. No nation has the means to challenge us. We can exert overwhelming power virtually anywhere we choose and in whatever cause we see fit.

Yet this is an ambiguous victory. Although our military power is unchallenged, it cannot easily be translated into the political goals we seek. We destroyed the Iraqi army in 1991, yet Saddam Hussein remained in power. We fed the hungry in Somalia, but retreated in disorder after interfering in the power struggle of rival clans. We deplored the ethnic violence in the former Yugoslavia, but had no solution for a conflict rooted in ancient enmities.

What the end of the Cold War taught us is that the weapons we forged to fight it are virtually irrelevant once the battle is over. We are facing a problem we had not anticipated: that of translating military might into political power. We can bomb or blockade such places as Serbia, or Haiti, or North Korea. But we cannot impose our political will so easily.

The Cold War was dangerous, wasteful, obsessive, and at times irrational. Tens of thousands of lives were sacrificed in battles that we can hardly understand, let alone justify, today. Yet at least we could define what the Cold War was ostensibly about. The United States sought to restrain, and ultimately reverse, the military reach and political influence of the Soviet Union. Officials told us that if this were done, the major cause of violence in the world would be removed.

But the world after the Cold War is even more violent, yet without a single cause. We were no more prepared for this than we were for the abrupt and unexpected end of the Cold War. Although we devoted an enormous part of our national resources, as well as our emotional and intellectual energies, into fighting the

Soviets, we never seriously thought about what the political landscape might be after battle. Many of us simply assumed that the world would return to something like normal.

But of course there was no normal. Europe had not been normal since 1914. War, revolution, depression, then war again had obliterated the boundaries and the common civilization of the self-confident societies that had existed before World War I. When communist authority collapsed in 1990, with it went the whole structure of postwar Europe. In the east, the former communist states were no longer sullen and orderly, but fearful and disorderly. Whereas they had once blamed distant "imperialists" for their troubles, they now turned on ethnic minorities in their own midst. In the west of the continent, where the wealthy and secure had built a European "community," the dream of unity was shaken by the realization that the very notion of Europe, as it had been understood for half a century, was a creation of the Cold War. That conception would have to be redefined—and in a way that threatened long-cherished assumptions.

In Asia, too, there was no normal. Before the Cold War set the stage for new alliances, Japan was a defeated imperial nation and China an impoverished and exploited colony. Today Japan has become rich and economically powerful, and China has embarked on a path of industrialization and militarization that is making it a major global player.

While the end of the Cold War has resolved some problems, it has unleashed others we had not anticipated—problems that have no simple military solution.

The "captive nations" of Eastern Europe, whose liberation we ritualistically demanded in Congressional resolutions, are now our problem—and that of the West Europeans—rather than Moscow's. Our NATO allies, who used to berate us for being domineering and "hegemonic," now complain even more loudly that we do not care about them anymore. Whereas we once protected them from the Soviets, they now want us to protect them from one another. And Russia—our Cold War nemesis—is today a problem not because of its strength but because of its weakness. A weak Russia cannot provide stability or prosperity for its citizens. It cannot impose order on the violent tribes along its frontiers. And it cannot ensure the strong centralized control over nuclear weapons on which our own security depends. Ironically, a Russian threat to commit suicide today seems more dangerous than an earlier one to commit aggression.

The Third World, where we fought the most vicious battles of the Cold War—sometimes with proxy armies, as in Angola, Nicaragua, and Afghanistan—has now become politically irrelevant. The communist country whose unification we fought so hard, and destroyed so much to prevent—Vietnam—has traded the teachings of Karl Marx for those of Adam Smith. And after viewing it as a willing tool of Chinese imperialism, we now have come to appreciate it as a useful counter to China.

Finally, Japan, whose economy we restored so that it could play its role in the integrated global market that our policymakers were intent on creating, has succeeded all too well. It has today achieved by commerce what it tried to do half a century ago by war: its Greater East Asian Co-prosperity Sphere. It has done this with our help. We spared it the expense of paying for its own defense against its communist neighbors, and we provided the lucrative markets for it to service our military operations in Korea and Vietnam. We now hold contentious summit conferences with the Japanese, just as we used to do with the Russians. And Americans tell pollsters that, with the Soviet Union gone, they consider Japan to be our most formidable rival.

It is not surprising that there are those, particularly in the foreign policy elite, who actually miss the Cold War. It gave us a cause to defend, allies that paid deference, and a role as undisputed boss of the realm we called the "free world." No wonder that we do not celebrate its end, as we do that of earlier wars.

Soviet communism, for all its evils, held in check the explosive nationalism of Eastern Europe and the old Soviet republics. It also enabled the superpowers to control their more unruly Third World clients. The Soviet Union almost certainly would not have allowed its client, Saddam Hussein, to have attacked Kuwait, thus provoking the Americans to send an army to the Gulf.

Nor would Washington have tolerated the banditry that led to mass starvation in its former "strategically located" Cold War base in Somalia.

In its perverted way, the Cold War was a force for stability. By dividing Germany it resolved, for a time, the perennial problem of preventing it from dominating Europe. It smothered the ethnic rivalries of the old Romanov, Ottoman, and Hapsburg empires that have now emerged with such fury. It slowed down the dispersion of nuclear weapons to ambitious states. And it ensured the status of the superpowers.

The Cold War also offered a structure for understanding the world. It was a struggle not only for power and influence, but for the minds of men everywhere. As an alternative to our own messianic ideology of market democracy, communism posed a challenge to what we were and what we espoused.

The Cold War world seemed neatly divided between democracy and totalitarianism, with the shades of gray wiped out. To the sordid and self-serving politics of statecraft, and to alliances of convenience, it provided a comforting note of moral certainty.

Now, with the battle over, the lines between good and evil are once again fuzzy. It used to be that a regime had only to invoke the specter of communism to be showered with American aid and protection. But without communism the issues are more complex, and also less compelling.

Should we become involved if a government founders? Why? Because a state is democratic? Capitalist? A good market? A source of supplies? Or simply needy? We espouse principles like democracy and freedom. But where should we apply them? Can we apply them? And if so, at what price?

During the Cold War it was all so easy. Whatever was wrong in the world was the fault of communism. We had an enemy and we had a crusade. Now we are alone: a superpower without a challenger, a crusader without a mission.

What happened to our enemy? For decades our leaders warned that this evil, yet somehow seductive, force was poised to take over the world. They led us to wars in remote and seemingly insignificant places for reasons that were often as difficult for them to explain as for us to understand. Yet in the end there was no colossus: only an inept, strife-ridden, and impoverished regime—a gigantic Potemkin village.

What were we so afraid of? Indeed, were our leaders really afraid of the power of the Soviets to seduce and intimidate the entire world? Or did they find it to be a useful enemy that allowed them to build up the military and economic power that created what has been justly called the American Century?

Future historians will ask why we felt so vulnerable—far more so than the Europeans, who were within walking distance of the Red Army. The answer lies partly in our long history of geographic invulnerability. The protection of vast oceans produced an exaggerated sense of security that we came to take as a birthright. The answer also lies in the struggle with an ideology so alien to our own, yet seemingly so seductive to many.

Unlike World War II, which for the United States was a four-year state of emergency with a clear beginning and a triumphant military conclusion, the Cold War was a permanent crisis. With the nuclear stalemate, it could not be resolved in military battle, and it was hard to foresee how or when it would ever end. Generations came and went, while the Cold War continued.

Inevitably the Cold War came to dominate our thinking, just as it did the national agenda. It defined our government and how we lived our lives. We even used it to justify our own domestic activities to ourselves. When the government provided aid to school children, it called the program the "National Defense Education Act." When it built the interstate highway system, it labeled it the "National Defense Highway Act."

Until the inauguration of Bill Clinton in 1993, every president since Franklin Roosevelt has been preoccupied with foreign policy. Some—like John Kennedy, Richard Nixon, and George Bush—seemed to view the nation's domestic problems as annoying distractions from the excitement and dangers of global crises. Foreign policy always came first. How we lived with each other—whether we were rich or poor, segregated or integrated, united or divided—always came second. This, too, we came to take as natural and proper: at least until the nation swayed near the breaking point in the

1960s over yet another foreign policy adventure—our war in Vietnam.

■ ■ ■

The Cold War, despite its enormous cost and waste, was in some ways good for the United States. Government contracts and payrolls ensured generations of prosperity, American industry for a time dominated what came to be a global marketplace, the nation's institutions and attitudes broadened out to the world, and our cultural reach became pervasive.

Throughout the world America's influence has been profound, particularly upon the young. They equate exports of American culture—whether as clothing, entertainment, leisure, generational identities, or the rationalization of time itself—with the very concept of modernization. To be a person of the second half of the twentieth century has meant, to some extent, to have made an accommodation to American culture.

Coupled with these factors is an expansive energy that has impelled Americans to export to the world the qualities and conditions we value for ourselves. Americans have always been salesmen, and the Cold War gave us the opportunity to provide so much of what the world seemed to want: economic help, military protection, and political solidarity.

And then there is democracy, the export product that Americans seem to care about most. Its adoption by others, at least rhetorically, is treated not only as a tribute to America, but as an endorsement of the nation itself. Our version of democracy, most Americans are convinced, is the model to which all less advantaged peoples aspire.

The Soviet Union also had its global export. Communism was a powerful ideology that offered to millions an explanation of the inequitable conditions of a seemingly arbitrary world. It was particularly appealing to the aspiring leaders of Third World states newly aroused to self-assertion and nationalism.

In one sense, the Soviet Union was hardly an inspiring example of liberation. From its very inception its leaders adopted a distorted version of Marxism that was used to justify the most abject tyranny against their own people. The corruptions of Soviet communism were revealed in the purges and gulags of the 1930s and the repressions imposed upon Eastern Europe during the Cold War.

Yet the ideology itself—and the verbal, if sometimes hypocritical, allegiance of Soviet leaders to it—was appealing as an alternative to those, especially in the Third World, whose historical experience had given them reason to associate capitalism with exploitation.

This roused American leaders to a global contest fought for the highest stakes. Communism provided the counterideology that activated the powerful American sense of mission. This was utilized by leaders to justify what might otherwise have seemed a more mundane power struggle between two continental states with global ambitions. Ronald Reagan's description of the

Soviet Union as an "evil empire" was perfectly suited to the political theology of the Cold War.

Because so much of the contest was bound up in ideology, the collapse of Soviet communism meant far more than simply a truce in the American–Soviet competition. Such a description implies merely a struggle of nations. Rather, the Cold War was viewed as a contest between "alternative ways of life," as President Harry Truman labeled it in enunciating what became known as his doctrine.

These ways of life challenged each other to serve as the model for mankind. When one collapsed, the other, having been deprived of its antithesis, lost much of its missionary fervor. With Soviet-style communism discredited, and indeed with the Soviet Union gone, it suddenly mattered much less whether Third World nations adopted American-style democratic capitalism. What once seemed a vital, even a deadly, interest now became a task for bureaucrats, bankers, and economists.

If both superpowers were expansionist, they were so in quite different ways. Communism is by its very nature a proselytizing ideology. It claims to be a culminating development in history and to bring about the liberation of mankind. By definition it is universalist and not the instrument of any single power. The very notion of "socialism in one country" was a betrayal of communism, as was the claim that the Soviet version of communism should take precedence over any other.

"Socialist internationalism" served as a pretext for

great power expansion by the Soviet Union. The ideology was employed in the service of the Soviet state. This does not necessarily mean that it was done so entirely cynically. Political leaders, too, are governed by their intellectual assumptions. For many, the glorification of the Soviet state was not incompatible with the expansion of communism. Indeed, for them the former was the instrument of the latter.

The United States, in its own way, also pursued a path of expansion during the Cold War. It did so with enormous gusto, and with the conviction that it was serving a larger purpose: the containment of a threat and the promulgation of a liberating idea. The nation's various interventions throughout the world, the governments it sustained or overthrew, the wars it fought in Asia, the high state of emergency and excitement that sustained these efforts—all this cannot be explained by any conventional notion of a security threat.

Was the United States likely to be any less safe if Marxist rather than anti-Marxist authoritarians controlled Angola? Or if communists extended their control over the southern part of Vietnam in 1965 rather than in 1975? Yet many billions of dollars and even many thousands of American lives were willingly spent as though such things mattered greatly.

What impelled policymakers to pursue such decisions? Part of the reason was the enormous power of the United States to make things happen. Nations that cannot reach so far are satisfied with less expansive ambitions, and with narrower definitions of their security. Because America's reach was global, so was its definition of security. Because we had the power to affect events nearly everywhere, we did not allow ourselves the luxury of ignoring things on the periphery. Whereas most nations define a "vital national interest" as something akin to a matter of life or death, for a nation as powerful as the United States it can be extended to minor inconveniences.

We could also intervene virtually at will across the globe, and fight two major wars in Asia, because the other nations that might normally have contained us—Japan, China, Germany—were in temporary eclipse. During the forty-odd years following World War II, Western Europe was preoccupied by reconstruction, Japan by getting rich, and China by civil war, Maoist purges, and modernization. None of these nations enjoyed the strength or marshaled the will seriously to challenge either the United States or the Soviet Union.

Yet many will object—and with reason—that the United States, unlike the Soviet Union, or even unlike more traditional great powers, did not intervene simply for self-serving purposes, but in defense of a noble idea. That idea, of course, is democracy. It is worth pondering that the United States is virtually alone in the world in declaring the promulgation of democracy to be a major foreign policy objective.

The long-standing and self-declared American crusade for democracy has three different aspects. The first is an affirmation of the political ideology of the United States. The nation "conceived in liberty" affirms its qualities by seeking to extend them to others—just as, for example, republican France did in the late eighteenth century by fostering revolutionary movements across Europe.

As with the young French Republic, this ambition expresses an inner compulsion of self-affirmation. It is the banner under which the nation asserts and legitimizes itself. It is what sets it apart from other less idealistic states. Yet its very essence is evangelical. Liberty is not merely a blessing to be savored privately, but a grace that must be spread to others.

It is proselytizing by nature. Thus the exportation of democracy, particularly in its capitalistic, free-market version, is an integral part of America's sense of mission. It is the way that the nation justifies to itself, as well as to others, the universality of its principles.

The second aspect of the crusade for democracy is the belief that a world of governments more like our own will be a safer and more prosperous one. Democratic governments, it is asserted, are less belligerent than authoritarian ones. This, it is said, makes them more amenable to negotiation and compromise. They are presumably less likely to resort to force—at least against one another. They do, of course, go to war against non-democratic ones, often in the name of democracy—as we have seen in our own Cold War interventions.

While the promotion of democracy is sometimes described as sentimental or idealistic, Tony Smith has argued strongly in a recent study that the "greatest ambition of United States foreign policy over the past century" has been "to foster democracy abroad as a way of ensuring national security."[1] If this be true, it is curious that officials choose to emphasize idealism rather than security as a justification for promoting democracy, whether by force or by example.

The third aspect of the crusade for democracy is its utility as justification for actions that might otherwise be considered unduly meddlesome, self-aggrandizing, or even belligerent. During the Cold War the United States intervened in the affairs of a great many nations—whether through invasion, coercion, or persuasion—to defend its interests as it saw them. But invariably they were said to be inspired by a concern for democracy.

To dismiss the ideal of democracy in U.S. foreign policy as essentially window-dressing would be a mistake. Its virtues are sincerely esteemed, even if imperfectly applied. Americans want to believe that their pursuits, whether public or private, are at heart virtuous. Avowedly Realpolitik diplomacy, of the kind normally practiced by Europeans (and in the Nixon administration so openly by Henry Kissinger), makes Americans uncomfortable. We are thrilled by its bravado, but disturbed by its cynicism.

We prefer to leaven power with principle, and are made uneasy when they come into conflict. This happened often enough during the Cold War. Yet then it could be resolved by a sense of threat and an appeal to self-interest. Now, with the Cold War behind us, the old clarity has given way to confusion and doubt. In part this contributes to what has been called Cold War nostalgia.

The Cold War was many things: a deadly struggle, an obsession, a vocation. It was also a competition in economic bankruptcy. In this the Soviets, being poorer, gave out first. But if the struggle destroyed them, it also weakened us: in our ability to compete with our allies, in meeting the needs of our people, in honoring our political values.

It will be difficult to find a way back from the Cold War. For it was more than merely an appendage to our society. It was its central focus for three generations. The American economy, its work force, its education and training, its films and literature, its myths and its dreams all focused on the Cold War. Whole professions and even states have been dependent on it.

The contest is over and the Cold War world has receded into the already-dim past. Yet it cannot be so easily exorcised. For the Cold War was only in part about America's contest with the Soviet Union. It was also about a role of dominance that the foreign policy elite sought to exert, and to which it is still committed even though the old foe is vanquished.[2]

Today we are at a turning point in our foreign policy in some ways comparable to that of 1946–1947. At that time, in the flush of victory—with Japan and Germany in ruins, Britain and France reduced to dependency, and the wartime alliance with the Soviet Union falling apart—the nation redefined its relationship with the world. The prewar policy of isolationism had become irrelevant, the old balance of power could not be reconstituted, and Moscow seemed threatening. From the foundation of American power, officials crafted a policy of sweeping scope.

Its twin anchors were containment and expansion: containment of Soviet territorial temptations through military and economic power; expansion through alliances, bases, investments, and bribes. This policy restrained Soviet ambitions and ushered in an era of dominance from Washington justly called the Pax Americana.

That era is now behind us, a casualty of the very success of containment and the economic recovery of Europe and Asia. Containment has become obsolete, and with it the enormous military apparatus constructed in its name. We are left with a doctrine deprived of its logic, and with a military force—capable of wiping out whole countries—without an objective commensurate with its power.

As the architects of the American Century did nearly half a century ago, we must reinvent American foreign policy for another postwar world. This means forging not only the mechanics and the superstructure, but the very terms of our relationship with other states—and beyond that, with ourselves.

Perhaps most crucial is the restructuring of the compact we Americans have with one another—our sense of who we are as a people, what we stand for, and how we can best live among others. For as long as most of us can remember, foreign policy has dominated our national agenda. Our domestic needs have consistently been sacrificed to it. We have turned security against foreign challengers into a shibboleth. But we have neglected the threats to our own security that come from within.

2

···

Interest and Morality

During the darkest days of the Cold War, parallels were sometimes drawn to World War I. Conflict, it was said, could break out, as it had in 1914, through miscalculation, rhetorical posturing, or technological dictates of the new weaponry. What almost no one imagined was that the Cold War might suddenly end in a way similar to the way it had ended on the eastern front in 1918: through the internal collapse and unconditional withdrawal of the Russians.

That one of the superpowers might simply retire from the contest, lose its empire, jettison its social system, and go into convulsions—all this seemed no less improbable early in this century than did the demise of its successor a few years ago.

The collapse of the Russian state, the Bolshevik seizure of power, and abject surrender to the Germans in 1918 did not happen without cause. These events stemmed from the rigidities of autocratic rule, the costs of fighting an interminable war, and the loss of faith by the nation's elite in the system itself. Afterwards, what once seemed unthinkable became strikingly obvious. Of course the Russian state, outwardly so formidable and unyielding, was merely a shell. It was almost inevitable, given the toll of war, that the ruling dynasty would fall. Was this not evident?

Yet it was not at all evident at the time because virtually no one in a position of power wanted to believe it. The British and French, needing a strong ally in their war against Germany, ignored the ominous signs of Russia's impending collapse. They believed what suited their purposes.

All this now seems abundantly clear. But are there not strong parallels between 1917–1918 and 1990–1991? In both cases political leaders were stunned by events in Russia for which their analyses and assumptions had not prepared them.

Imperial Russia was not the staunch ally that the Entente powers wanted. Nor was communist Russia as mighty an adversary as American policymakers thought: not in internal cohesion, not in military reach, and probably not in geopolitical ambitions. In a real sense the United States was engaged in a deadly struggle with a phantom Russia, just as Russian leaders—bedeviled by fear, suspicion, ambition, and ideology—were with a phantom America.

Despite George Kennan's hopeful belief in 1947 that "Soviet power, like the capitalist world of its conception, bears within it the seeds of its own decay, and that the sprouting of these seeds is well advanced,"[1] virtually no serious scholar, strategist, or political analyst in the late 1980s believed that the Cold War would end as it did—with the collapse of the Soviet empire in Europe, the dissolution of the Soviet state, and the repudiation of communism itself by those thought to be its most ardent adherents. Such a disaster normally results from a catastrophic defeat in war.

In fact, from a great power perspective, the Cold War was not supposed to have ended at all. The competition was supposed to have been regulated by the two super-powers. Detente, arms accords, rules of engagement would lessen the costs of maintaining their rival spheres of influence. The advantages that the Cold War seemed to offer both major contestants were so manifest that there was little incentive on either side to end it.

Yet end it suddenly did, and because the other side was simply too weak both within and without to sustain it. This requires us to question some of the assumptions on which American policy was based. Although Ronald Reagan correctly spoke in 1982 of a "great revolutionary crisis" in the Soviet Union "where the demands of the economic order are conflicting directly with those of the political order," and declared that this would "leave Marxism–Leninism on the ash heap of history,"[2] his administration did not behave as though it believed such a collapse to be imminent or clearly foreseeable. Under Reagan, U.S. spending rose to unprecedented peacetime levels and Third World interventions were intensified. It was only after the end of the Cold War that the administration publicly maintained that its strategy all along had been to drive the Soviets into bankruptcy.

However much we declared Soviet communism to be an aberration, we treated it as formidable and all but immutable. The enormous apparatus of government intelligence and spy operations, of subsidized think tanks and research institutes, and the entire discipline of "strategic studies" failed to prepare the ground for an understanding of what is arguably the most momentous political event of this century. In understanding the collapse of communism and the Soviet state, the supposed experts have been virtually irrelevant.

In part, this is a failure of American social science, with its blind faith in quantification, its indifference to history and culture, and its aggressive ethnocentrism. In a larger sense, it is also a failure of political intelligence, a failure to penetrate into the depths of an adversary society. American officials often saw the Soviet Union they wanted to see: a society of automatons mesmerized by a messianic ideology and intent on dominating the world.

The Soviet state, with its expansionist ideology and its repressive history, was more complicated than that. So was the United States. After World War II American policymakers wanted to block a retreat to prewar passivity and to engage the nation's formidable energies in a global vocation. Soviet brutality in Eastern Europe, combined with the appeal of communist ideology to millions, provided the challenge that permitted a sweeping engagement, and a global extension, of American power. And it supplied the domestic consensus that made it possible.

The Cold War also reorganized the structure of our society. It transformed a highly decentralized nation into an increasingly centralized one. Whereas major economic and political decisions were once made in scores of state capitals and major cities, they are now being made in Washington. They are not, however, always made by the government alone. Powerful corporations and special interest groups increasingly dictate the flow of power and money.

Just as the federal government became the nation's largest employer, so it was also the nation's largest contractor. It provided subsidies for defense industries, ensured that they would always make profits, decided what products they would manufacture, and determined how many people they would employ. Although we continued to call this capitalism, in effect it was back-door socialism—or perhaps more properly, corporatism: a collusion among big government, big industry, and big labor.

The Cold War exalted the cult of the expert and the manipulator. As government expanded to meet the demands of a wartime economy, so experts flocked to Washington. Suddenly there was a great demand for the specialized services of economists, strategists, and political analysts. Government officials out of a job because of a change in administration became consultants—or else lobbyists. Thus it was that hardly anyone ever needed to, or did, leave Washington.

The tidal waves of money flowing from Washington pushed up prices, drove down the value of the dollar, fueled an explosion of trading and speculation on stock exchanges, and helped create the culture of the Wall Street manipulator. Where the acquisition of wealth rested on power and influence, the insider was king. Washington and Wall Street were linked by a shuttle in more ways than one.

The Cold War vastly augmented the power of the presidency. War always enhances the authority of the ruler. This war was no exception. It allowed the President, despite Constitutional barriers, to lead the nation into war when and where and how he saw fit. Although long and costly wars were fought in Korea and Vietnam, no President ever sought the required formal declaration of war, nor did Congress insist upon it.

With the end of the Cold War, the tide has been reversed. Instead of laments about the "imperial presidency," we now complain about the absence of vigorous "leadership." We want our presidents to be assertive, but not to demand any sacrifices.

If the Cold War fueled scientific research, modernized social institutions, speeded the integration of ethnic and minority groups, furthered progressive goals, and broke down sectional differences, its demise—coupled with a weakening of presidential power—may cause serious problems of adjustment within the society.[3]

The Cold War also created a class of administrators to man the nation's global outposts and take over its new responsibilities. Like the European colonial powers before us, we developed a colonial service and staffed it with everyone from teachers to accountants. This army of administrators instructed people from Algeria to Zanzibar on how to plant crops, run (or overthrow) a government, and fight wars, often against their own citizens. Millions of American civilians worked overseas on U.S. government payrolls and soon developed a taste for it.

These civilians were, of course, augmented by our armed forces—including their numerous spouses and children. During the Cold War we had more than one million soldiers in thirty countries, organized four regional defense alliances, had mutual defense treaties with forty-two nations, and furnished military or economic aid to nearly a hundred countries around the globe. In effect, we created what most foreign observers describe as an empire. That we possessed such a Cold War empire is so taken for granted by the rest of the world as hardly to merit comment. We alone find this notion surprising.

Instead of viewing this empire as embarrassing, let us simply consider it a description of what has been, on the whole, a reasonably successful institution. It began in earnest after 1944, when we set the groundwork for an integrated global trading system with the dollar as the key currency. We pushed the British, Dutch, and French to liberate their colonies, and we then extended our economic and political—and sometimes military—umbrella to these newly independent lands.

We could afford the costs of such global engagement. Our factories and fields, unscarred by bombs, produced half the world's goods. The (then) almighty dollar became the universal denominator. This made New York the world's financial capital. It also allowed us to camouflage our debts by printing money that others, for a time, considered to be as "good as gold."

We rebuilt Western Europe and Japan to create a global market system that produced great wealth for the industrialized countries involved. In return for protection, our allies, albeit somewhat grudgingly, allowed us to negotiate for them with the Russians and conduct whatever activities we chose in the Third World. They also bought our Treasury IOUs, thus allowing us to import more of their goods than our labors would otherwise permit.

But in the early 1970s things started to go wrong. First there was Vietnam, which demonstrated—as the British, French, Portuguese, and Dutch had learned—that it is easier to acquire a colony than hold on to it. The United States lost the Vietnam war not because of the media or the antiwar movement. The former was more timid and the latter less effective than the rewriters of history would have us believe. It lost because the American public—divided between those who wanted victory and those who wanted out—could no longer be persuaded to support a stalemate that was corroding America itself.

After Vietnam came the OPEC-enforced oil embargo

of 1973, which showed that we could be vulnerable to weak states as well, so long as they had something that we wanted badly. Military muscle began to be restrained by economic balance sheets. The huge military buildup under Reagan produced a great deal of new hardware, but also quadrupled the national debt. The hardware is now rusting, but we will be paying the debt for generations.

Today the very notion of the American Empire has a plaintive ring. Like the Wild West, one can imagine it as an attraction at some future Disney theme park. The real empire, the one that made friend and foe stand up and salute, is quickly passing into memory. It is a victim both of historical change and of an economy that bent under the burden. One of the anomalies of our empire is that we were hardly aware of its existence before we had to cope with the consequences of its demise.

But there need be little cause for regret. The truth is that empire is an expensive business. It is acquired in a frenzy of exuberance, milked for a time in the soft glow of self-satisfaction (the French had their *mission civilisatrice,* the British their "white man's burden"), and then paid for, like many of the fruits of adolescent enthusiasm, with sweat and treasure.

Our foreign policy during the Cold War would have been more successful, and also less costly, had it confined itself to its supposed goal: the containment of Soviet military power. Moscow's enforced control over Eastern Europe, its potential threat to Western Europe and

Japan, and its arsenal of nuclear weapons needed to be checked. The United States was the only power fully capable of doing so.

The Cold War became global with the triumph of the Communists in China in 1949 and the expansion of the civil war in Korea the following year. This transformed the containment of Soviet military power in Europe— a relatively limited objective—into a struggle against what policymakers termed the "international communist conspiracy." It was fought almost entirely in the Third World, through proxy or semicolonial wars. And after the near-disaster of the Cuban missile crisis of 1962, both superpowers made sure that their forces never directly engaged one another.

The interesting question about the Cold War is not why it ended as it did, but why it lasted so long. Why did the superpowers, having worked out the ground rules of detente in the 1970s, not simply call a truce that would have spared them proxy wars and much of the burden of the arms race? Why did the West Europeans and the Japanese not use some of their newly earned wealth to gain military independence from their protector? Why did Moscow not try to outflank a hostile Beijing by wooing Tokyo? Why did the Americans not support, rather than fight, Vietnam in order to balance off China? Why did the United States, long after its own economic troubles set in, insist on paying the lion's share of its rich allies' defense costs?

There are a number of reasons why the Cold War

continued in its familiar grooves. First, the NATO Europeans and the Japanese did not want to take over their full defense burden from the Americans. They were intent on building their economies to emulate, and one day to rival, American economic power.

Second, both superpowers found certain advantages in maintaining hegemony over their allies. It extended their reach and increased their freedom of action. The Russians did this through the physical occupation and intimidation of Eastern Europe; the Americans by providing for the defense of Western Europe and Japan.

Third, America and Russia were too caught in the mechanics of their competition, the constraints of their rival ideologies, and the fears of declining status to work out a mutually beneficial modus vivendi. Thus they fought costly wars on Third World terrains of little intrinsic value, such as Vietnam and Afghanistan, weakening themselves in the process.

Fourth, there were considerable advantages for both superpowers in the Cold War system, grotesquely wasteful and economically irrational though it was. For the Russians it ensured a free hand in the occupied satellites of Eastern Europe, kept the Germans physically divided and politically in check, and endowed superpower status on a country whose civilian economy was more akin to the Third World than the First. For the United States it guaranteed both military dominance and political leverage over such potential rivals as Germany and Japan, fortified the domestic economy with infusions of military spending, and allowed the smooth functioning of the integrated global market economy that was the goal of America's postwar planners.

Thus to many it seemed, as one skeptical observer has written, that the goal of each superpower "was not so much victory over the other as maintenance of a balance."[4]

■ ■ ■

If during the Cold War Americans came to take global intervention for granted, they nonetheless have been highly ambivalent about its scope and even its justification. The postwar triumph of internationalism over a deep-seated isolationism has not been total, and the tension between the two is powerful, if submerged.

The isolationist impulse rests on two powerful forces: first, the deeply felt belief in American exceptionalism; and second, the unique geographical position of the United States which has, until the nuclear age, conferred a profound sense of security from foreign quarrels.

American exceptionalism is rooted in the conviction that the United States, created as an alternative to the tyrannous regimes of Europe, would retain its republican and humanistic values by strict separation from the intrigues of the Old World. Herein lay the counsel of George Washington in his Farewell Address, and of John Quincy Adams, who warned against involvement in "all the wars of interest and intrigue, of individual avarice, envy and ambition, which assume the colors and usurp the standards of freedom."

Independence meant full control over the nation's

destiny. America, in Adams's words, would "recommend the general cause [of liberty] by the countenance of her voice, and by the benignant sympathy of her example." It would be an exemplar to the world rather than a dabbler in its sordid rivalries.

However, intermingled with this belief in purity through separation was an equally powerful one: that America had an obligation to spread the blessings of freedom. This missionary impulse, which drove church ministers to convert the "heathens" of China and other unfortunate lands to the blessings of Christianity and capitalism, also took a political form. Salvation would be found not merely by protecting and improving the nation, but by spreading democracy throughout the world.

Although it is said that the business of America is business, it is equally true that the ideology of America is democracy. Whether liberal or conservative, Americans share a profound belief that our system of government is not only best for us, but best for peoples everywhere. Indeed, it is almost as though we sought to validate our system to ourselves by converting the entire world to it.

To many foreigners, the promulgation of democracy is often viewed as an excuse for American expansion. General de Gaulle in his memoirs charged that the energetic nation that sought "to help those who were in misery or bondage the world over, yielded in her turn to that taste for intervention in which the instinct for domination cloaked itself."

But where foreigners see expansion, Americans see

philanthropy. As usual, Woodrow Wilson expressed this best. In his war message to Congress of April 1917 he declared that the United States would enter the European conflict "for democracy, for the right of those who submit to authority to have a voice in their own government, for the rights and liberties of small nations . . . and to make the world itself free."

Such statements are often considered to be either naive or hypocritical. But they should not be dismissed so easily. They are deeply felt and serve an important purpose. They affirm the concerns of a nation that, although settled as a European colony, had to create its own identity as something different from, and better than, the societies from which the colonists had fled.

Beyond that, the colonists had to justify the actions they took to secure that identity. The generations that succeeded the colonists had to weave myths to deal with the harsh and often brutal realities of creating a nation. They had to find a way of coming to terms with the virtual extermination by white settlers of the native peoples of North America, and with the commercial traffic in human beings that was slavery.

That uniquely American art form—the Western—deals precisely with the great issue of the subduing of the continent and its inhabitants. The "winning of the West" was defined as a struggle for civilization against the "forces of savagery." The morality of Westerns lies in the utilization of terrible force as the means to the attainment of a higher purpose.

In this sense the American film hero is a lonely fighter for civilization, for society, for virtue. He uses harsh means to achieve good, employs force not for its own sake but for a morally higher goal. He is Superman, Shane, or the Terminator, wielding power not for himself but to help others. Often he is a bit naive and overly trusting, yet his moral purpose is clear.

Contrast this with James Bond, the amoral hero of British spy dramas. Contemptuous of any ideals or loyalties, Bond is an elegant hired cynic. Ostensibly on "Her Majesty's service," his only values are those of power and prestige, and his only interests those of pleasure. He is the supreme individualist, the rogue killer unbounded by oath or loyalty. Bond is the sybaritic and cynical European; Superman the puritanical and idealistic American.

Despite the powerful missionary impulse of Americans, we have, until the Cold War, been reluctant to go abroad, in the younger Adams's celebrated phrase, "in search of monsters to destroy." The American public is essentially inward-looking. It is preoccupied by the internal issues of American society, and has been accustomed to do so by a long history of detachment from dynastic foreign quarrels.

The great distance of the United States from Europe and Asia, as well as from the continent of South America, has spared it from invasion, conquest, and even extensive cultural interaction with dangerous rivals. For the United States, during much of its history, foreign affairs was a choice, not a necessity; an opportunity, not a danger.

No wonder that to this day so many Americans feel ambivalent about the intensity of American political involvement with other countries, or why they often view this as a distraction from the needs of the domestic society. American leaders have found in self-interest reasons why such involvement may be necessary. But to sell this to a skeptical public they have often packaged it as altruism. Indeed, they have sometimes even seemed to perceive it that way themselves.

Thus the American public has been told that the American wars of the past half century, in Korea and Vietnam, were not in fact what they so patently seemed to others—efforts to retain regional hegemony, or ideological crusades based on an ignorance of history—but something more noble. They were presented as gifts of democracy to beleaguered peoples. Similarly, less costly interventions in various parts of the Third World were described as altruistic activities.

Being told that they were, at great cost, extending a favor, it is not surprising that Americans expected some appreciation for their assistance. Perhaps this is a partial explanation of the much-commented need of Americans to be liked. We want to be liked because we assume, and indeed have been told, that we are doing good. When the favor is not appreciated, we are puzzled at such ingratitude, and ultimately annoyed. It is at this point that we either go home, as in the case of Somalia, or wreak a terrible vengeance on those we are ostensibly helping, as in Vietnam.

The job of the foreign policy elite in the United States is more difficult than in most democratic societies. Unlike other nations, where foreign policy is viewed as the prerogative of a privileged class, every American feels that his views must be taken into account, and looks on experts with suspicion. For this reason, political leaders must produce elaborate justifications for American involvement in foreign quarrels.

These justifications may rest on self-interest, altruism, or ideology. The involvements that follow from them may be full-scale wars, as in Korea and Vietnam; quick invasions, as in Grenada and Panama; engineered coups d'etat, as in Guatemala and Iran; or war by proxy, as in Nicaragua and Angola. Even when they are quite limited, they are promoted with all the subtlety of the launching of a new detergent. A democracy like the United States does not enjoy the luxury of an unobtrusive foreign policy.

During the Cold War, when the sense of physical danger—manifested by the nuclear confrontation—was real, the public supported an interventionist foreign policy. It did so because it believed that there was no alternative. The only times the public seriously balked was in the two wars of "containment"—Korea and Vietnam—when the policy went out of control and lost touch with political reality.

At those times the belief that the nation's leaders had

broken faith with the public, and even with the national interest, was widespread. There was public pressure—especially during the most violent years of the Vietnam war—to retrench from seemingly indiscriminate overseas interventions. The foreign policy elite naturally decried these sentiments as "isolationist."

As a general rule, liberals tend to be sympathetic to big government and to military engagement in the service of noble causes. This is because they see government as an agent of reform, and they favor the spread of American values. Conservatives, by contrast, have traditionally favored weak government and have supported intervention only when required by security and self-interest.

The Cold War confused this dichotomy. Because the Soviets and their ideological allies espoused communism, conservatives urged intervention against them. Since this generally meant propping up right-wing, and often repressive, regimes, liberals were against it. The traditionally anticommunist right became interventionist, while the left flirted with what its critics called neoisolationism.

Now that the Cold War is over and communists are no more, the old categories are back in place: conservatives have lost their enthusiasm for intervention, while liberals have found reasons to celebrate it.

Let us consider the war in Bosnia as illustration. There the formerly antiwar left, which had ardently inveighed against U.S. support of the independence of South

Vietnam, now demanded U.S. military action to defend the independence of Bosnia. Conservatives, by contrast, not finding communists involved, declared that they could discern no "vital interest" to merit engagement. A similar divide occurred on the issue of invading Haiti to impose democracy.

Beneath the infinitely complex calibrations of "national interest" so favored by policy analysts lie elements of a morality tale. Most Americans, and particularly liberals, are not comfortable with the use of force against weaker nations unless some element of justice or morality seems to be involved. Thus George Bush, in preparing his war for cheap oil, had to pretend that saving the palaces of the Kuwaiti royal family was also a blow for righteousness. Even when we know that self-interest is involved, we like to believe that our use of force is reserved for virtuous causes.

When we are so persuaded, we are quite impervious to criticisms of foreign, or even domestic, critics. For example, the accusation (particularly during the Vietnam war) that U.S. intervention was "imperialistic" had virtually no effect on the American public. This was for the simple reason that most people believed that such a costly effort to help a besieged nation to guard its independence and practice democracy could not, by definition, be imperialistic.

Foreign critics, especially those operating within the confines of a Marxist vocabulary, never understood this. In denouncing "American imperialism" they would employ as motivation such economic concerns as cheap labor, exploitation of natural resources, and the like. But whatever the economic component, it was far less significant than the psychological and historical ones that govern the American political character.

American foreign policy in the Cold War period, and even far earlier, cannot be understood without addressing the underlying economic goals of policymakers. Yet an explanation of American diplomacy that rests entirely on economics is just as inadequate as one that ignores it.

The oscillation between isolation and intervention, the persistent emphasis on morality, the obsession with freedom and democracy, the relentless proselytization—none of this can be stuffed entirely into an economic straitjacket. Foreign policy elites have their priorities. But they must be blended into the concerns, the dreams, the myths, the passions, and the historical experience of the American public. U.S. foreign policy may often be naive or hypocritical. At times it is certainly self-defeating. But it cannot be confined to a balance sheet.

The Cold War bonded together interest and morality in a way that secured for a succession of presidents the support of the American people over a period of three generations. In a real sense, all the presidents from Franklin Roosevelt to George Bush—from 1940 to 1992—have been war presidents. Their authority as commanders-in-chief consistently overcame the doubts and criticisms of their domestic policies. Whenever they seemed to fail at home—as they all did in one way or another—a foreign crisis (and during the Cold War there was always such a crisis somewhere) usually restored their support and authority.

Bill Clinton is the first truly peacetime president in half a century. He has suffered from the inability to use a foreign threat to buttress his authority at home. The dilemma for him, and his successors, is that of forging a new foreign policy that can win public support by combining, as the Cold War did, interest and morality.

3

■ ■ ■

Finding a Role

More than forty years ago
Dean Acheson, in retirement as secretary of state, lectured the British that they had "lost an empire but not
yet found a role." The United States, he made it clear,
had taken over their old role of being the world's chief
banker, umpire, and police enforcer. Now it was up to
them to scale back their ambitions to accord with their
financial means.

His words were tough, but not inaccurate. British officials thought that he was rude, and spent the next decades trying to ignore the truth of his observation. What
Acheson was telling them was simply that the world had
moved on, other powers had come to the fore, and
though they were a great nation, they could no longer
run the show. They would have to adjust. Resisting the
reality of their altered situation, often filled with nos-
talgic bluster, they have been searching for a role ever
since.

Today we find ourselves in a similar situation. Yet unlike Britain in 1945, we have not been superseded by a more powerful challenger. It is not as though someone new has come along to beat us at the old game. If that were the case it might be enough simply to try harder. The problem is that the game itself has changed.

With the passing of the Cold War, the United States no longer enjoys either its old authority or its freedom of action. It needs the Europeans and Japanese, who were once so dependent on American protection, to buy the Treasury bonds that finance its persistent deficits. American presidents are loath to mount expensive military operations, as the Gulf war revealed, unless others help pay for them. And they do not want to get bogged down in open-ended "peacekeeping"—or, even less, "peace*making*"—forays into unruly regions unless others share responsibility, and also blame when things go awry.

If the end of the Cold War has rendered old rivalries obsolete, it has done the same for old power equations as well. Military might is now only one component of national power, and not nearly as great a one as it used to be. While the president can call out the army or unleash the CIA, these are not likely to be of much help in reducing Japanese trade barriers or taming the deficit.

The forum of competition among the major powers has, at least for the time being, moved from the military to the economic realm. It is no longer fought over pretensions of ideology, no longer governed by delicate military balances, and no longer conducted through military interventions. Increasingly it is one of technology, finance, trade, and innovation. In this realm we have seen old foes, like Russia, become alarmingly weak dependents, while our Cold War allies are becoming increasingly formidable trade rivals.

This dramatic shifting of the world power balance will not be easy for an American economy distorted by a half century of reliance on military spending, nor for an American public now deprived of an enemy to serve as reason for its sacrifices. Above all it will not be easy for American political elites which had come to take for granted that they had both the right and the duty to lead the rest of the world.

With the demise of our Soviet adversary and the breakdown of the old alliances, we are, in one sense, reverting to earlier patterns of international life: regional wars, power balances, coalitions, and spheres of influence. At the same time, traditional cultural and economic barriers among nations are being steadily eroded as an embryonic international society takes form.

The fragmentation of what only a few years ago seemed to be a politically stable, if divided, world is proceeding with frightening speed. The Cold War has given way, on the one hand, to an ever more integrated global economy of industrialized nations, and on the other hand to an ancient political primitivism marked by blood feuds, systemic breakdowns, and even wars of all against all.

Everywhere the nation-state is under assault—either from those who consider it anachronistic and would merge it into larger entities, such as the Europeans are attempting, or from those who decry it as a prison of tribes and nationalities and would smash it into ethnically "purer" parts. Sometimes in a single place both movements are going on simultaneously.

Yet even as the old order crumbles, the United States, from a military point of view, has never been more secure. For the first time in half a century we face no serious security threat from abroad. We are as near to being invulnerable as a nation can get. "There are no significant hostile alliances," Republican hopeful and former defense secretary Dick Cheney has stated. "The strongest and most capable countries in the world remain our friends."

Yet policymakers continue to be preoccupied by notions of threat and credibility. Even Bill Clinton, who cut his political teeth on opposition to the Vietnam war, periodically succumbs to the Cold War vocabulary. In announcing the American withdrawal from the ill-fated expedition to Somalia, he declared that it must be gradual and, in effect, disguised as a victory. Otherwise, he explained, "our own credibility with friends and allies would be damaged" and "our leadership in world affairs would be undermined."[1]

The term "credibility" once meant that we wanted the Russians to take our resolve seriously, lest they miscalculate and set a dire train of actions in motion: like the Cuban missile crisis. What does it mean today—and directed toward friends and allies? "Credibility" was ostensibly what we were trying to demonstrate in Vietnam.

The notion of credibility, like that of leadership, is linked to the way that the foreign policy establishment defines security. By "national security" it means not merely the physical protection of the nation, or the welfare and liberties of its citizens. Beyond that it means the defense of what it calls a "security environment." The special quality of such an environment is that it can be defined as big as one wishes. In the vagueness of the term lies its utility.

The environment can be one's own country, or the countries that surround it, or the countries and even oceans and air spaces that lie beyond that, or, for that matter, the entire world. A security environment, if defined large enough, embraces everything. This is what happened during the Cold War when the United States, facing a challenger of global ambitions, constructed a global definition of its own security.

Yet we were not the first to define security by the length of our reach or the depths of our pockets. The Victorians, as two British historians have recounted in a masterly study of the British Empire,[2] started out with the intention of protecting their core interests overseas. Yet the defense of their colonies inevitably drew them into ever-wider circles of engagement.

To protect their investments in India they had to

guard the Himalayas and the frontiers of Central Asia. To ensure safe transit for their ships they had also to control the Suez Canal. This meant policing Egypt, on whose soil the Canal was located, and the nearby countries of the Middle East, which could pose potential problems for the Canal. Ultimately, as the concentric rings grew ever-larger, this drew them as far afield as the east coast and even the interior of Africa.

Unfortunately the peoples of these areas were not always content with British rule. This obliged the British to police them, and also to provide benefits that would keep the natives happy. They became policemen imposing order on these areas, and eventually in lands adjacent to them, from which disorder spilled.

Soon they were engaged in tribal conflicts in the heart of Africa—ostensibly to protect their position in India. Since each link was considered vital, the chain got longer and longer until they were running an African empire.

In the end they never felt secure, no matter how much they controlled. The "frontiers of insecurity," in the historians' telling phrase, expanded indefinitely. It was governed not by any explicit definition of vital interest—nothing they could explain coherently to a concerned citizen. Rather it was governed by the ability of imperial England, then at the height of its pride and wealth, to project power.

Small nations, by contrast, take a more parsimonious approach to threats than do great ones. They first define their interests narrowly. Then they respond to situations which are threatening to those interests. The Swedes, for example, are greatly concerned with hostile submarines in the Baltic and have impressive measures to deal with them. They are not at all troubled by the political complexions of warring factions in Southeast Asia.

Powerful nations such as ours, particularly when they define themselves as "superpowers," are different. They turn the equation around. They perceive all unwelcome changes as threats. Then they declare that their "interests" require them to counter such "threats."

The result is to make interests universal. This was a hallmark of the American approach to the Cold War. Places became "crisis areas" when their governments were under attack from the left, or when their rulers threatened to "go communist" unless "saved" by large infusions of American dollars and military equipment. Under this definition, dozens, and even scores, of nations were deemed to be "vital" to our interests, and to some of them, such as South Korea and South Vietnam, we even sent our soldiers to fight in their wars.

■ ■ ■

During the Cold War the ultimate threat, however broadly defined, was the Soviet Union. This was what dictated most of our military strategy, the mission of our forces, the size of our defense budgets. When it disappeared, the logic of the strategy went with it. A new blueprint for American strategy had to be devised. Naturally it was assumed that, in the absence of an enemy, defense budgets would shrink and that there would be a "peace dividend."

In the fall of 1993 the Pentagon produced what it called a "bottom up" review of U.S. defense plans. Frankly admitting that, with the demise of communism, "the threat . . . is gone," it recognized that "in the post Cold War period perhaps [the] most important set of dangers that U.S. strategy must confront is economic."[3]

Nonetheless, the planners were willing to cut less than seven percent from the five-year force plan devised during the Cold War. They would make some cuts in the army, but increase the size of the Marines, and retain twelve aircraft carrier battle groups originally designed to keep open sea lanes, even though, in the document's words, "without the Soviet navy, no one challenges us for control of the seas."

To provide what it calls "reassurance" for Cold War allies, the Clinton administration, like the Bush administration before it, plans to keep at least 100,000 American troops in Europe and maintain forces permanently in Korea, Japan, and the Persian Gulf. Some $90 billion a year is earmarked for the protection of Gulf potentates—a sum that raises serious questions about the real price of "cheap" oil.

While the current defense budget of $253 billion is down fractionally from the previous year, it is still 85 percent of the average Cold War level. This makes it as large as that of all the other nations of the world *combined*.[4] Of the total, about half is geared for the defense of Cold War allies in Europe and Asia against the now-defunct Soviet Union.

Given the collapse of the nation that inspired the military budgets of the Cold War, what justifies them now? According to the Pentagon planners, it is the threat of "aggression by major regional powers with interests antithetical to our own," or smaller conflicts driven by "ethnic or religious animosities." To cope with such potential problems, the planners propose that the United States "be able to win two major regional conflicts that occur nearly simultaneously."

Which particular regional conflicts does the Pentagon have in mind? One possibility is a threat to the oil kingdoms. But neither Iran nor Iraq, the leading candidates, is a major power, and the greatest danger to the ruling families of these countries comes from dissidents bearing the Koran. Another area of contention is the two Koreas. Yet even should North Korea develop nuclear weapons, South Korea remains covered by the American nuclear guarantee. Should conventional war break out again, South Korea has more than ample manpower to deal with its northern cousins: it has twice the population of the North and ten times the wealth. In any case, rather than war between the two Koreas we will more likely see reunification, with the South taking over the North (and its nuclear capacity) just as West Germany took over the East.

Since the nations of Europe are more secure from aggression than they have been in sixty years, and since neither Russia nor any Asian power challenges vital American interests, it is hard to refute the conclusion of one analyst that the Pentagon's "planning 'requirements' have been invented to justify the forces and structures we have rather than to cope with the world we face." Indeed, this view seems to be supported, however inadvertently, even by defense secretary William Perry. In presenting the new strategy to the House armed services committee in the spring of 1994, he suggested that the Congressmen not fret about a gap between the two-war strategy and our ability to execute it, since "it's an entirely implausible scenario that we'd fight two wars at once."[5]

Why do we need Cold War defense budgets when there is no more Cold War? One answer lies, of course, in the desire of bureaucracies to defend and perpetuate themselves. The military is no different in this regard than private industry or any other branch of government. It is well known that the first law of bureaucracy is survival.

Yet the rationale can also be found in politics and strategy. The Cold War was not merely a struggle against communism, but an international system. The United States dominated that system through a network of regional alliances. Other industrialized nations that might have been tempted to act independently instead chose to defer to Washington. In an age of contending superpowers it was prudent to ally with the strongest and most friendly.

Absent a menacing enemy, that alliance system is difficult to maintain. Countries like Japan, China, and Germany have the potential to be major military powers. This would not only threaten American leadership, but (at least theoretically) increase the possibility of regional conflict in Europe and Asia.

What does this have to do with the U.S. defense budget? Everything. This is because political strategists have all along been concerned not only with containing communism, but with creating an integrated global system, resting on a political and an economic base, orchestrated from Washington. The end of the Cold War has loosened the cement holding that system together, but not its underlying rationale.

That rationale was made explicit in a Pentagon planning document that was leaked to the press in 1992. In blunt language, not intended for a general audience, its authors argued that the United States must "discourage the advanced industrial nations from challenging our leadership or even aspiring to a larger regional or global role."

The explanation for this immodest ambition is that any effort by other industrialized nations, even friendly ones, to exert more influence in their regions might lead to competition and strife with their neighbors. This could cause political instability, inhibit the flow of global trade, and upset a host of cooperative international agreements.

Thus the argument is that American hegemony is ultimately good for everyone, even though it may involve a heavy burden for the United States. This is ostensibly America's duty. Or as the Pentagon strategists argue, the United States must "retain the preeminent responsibility for addressing . . . those wrongs which threaten not only our interests, but those of allies or friends, or which could seriously unsettle international relations."[6]

This is at least part of the explanation of a paradox: why the end of the Cold War does not mean the end of Cold War military budgets, or why the disappearance of the Soviet Union and the conversion of China to capitalism presumably do not reduce the specter of global threats.

Whereas the American arsenal was once directed primarily against the Soviet Union, it would now be directed against everybody. Whereas it was once intended to contain communism, its goal now is nothing less than the containment of global disorder. If communism could at least be localized, disorder is epidemic everywhere. Thus it is not surprising that it should require forces comparable to those used to hold off the Soviet Union. The suppression of disorder requires an enormous array of weapons capable of engagement against wrongdoers everywhere.

The suffocation of disorder—or, to use the new terminology, the creation of a "stable international environment"—has now replaced the out-of-date containment doctrine as the national security establishment's formula for the 1990s.

It was not easy for the Pentagon to explain to the Europeans and the Japanese why they must be discouraged from "challenging our leadership or even aspiring to a larger global or regional role." For this reason embarrassed officials later put out a sanitized version of the report. Yet the central argument remained in place. It was in everyone's interest that the United States smother conflict everywhere, and thereby ostensibly remove the need for other major powers to build up their armed forces.

There are a number of problems with this strategy, even in terms of its own dubious premises.

First, does the prosperity of the industrialized nations really depend on a tranquil international environment? History would seem to demonstrate the opposite. Nations are rarely so prosperous as when engaged in war or the preparation for war. Factories are humming full blast, unemployment lines disappear, contentious ethnic and social groups are joined in common purpose.

It was the Korean war and the subsequent rearmament drive that lifted the cloud of another depression from the American economy. That same war persuaded American occupation officials to remove the restrictions on Japanese cartels and war criminals so that they could provide the equipment the United States needed to fight in Korea. That in turn set in motion the reindustrialization that has become the Japanese juggernaut. Similarly, West Europe's economy moved into high gear with the launching of the Cold War.

Second, if we are the international cop on the beat, how do we decide which nation to protect? Let us assume that China and Japan get into a fight, or China and Russia. How do we decide which one should win? We trade with all of them. They trade with each other. When we take one side, we alienate the other. The alienated side will not see us as a friendly arbitrator, but as an enemy. It will not feel "reassured," but threatened. Instead of being a "regional balancer and honest broker," to use a Pentagon official's phrase, we will have become a meddlesome belligerent.

Third, why would any major nation turn over its military security—that is, the defense of its vital interests—to another nation in the absence of a compelling reason to do so? We certainly would not. No nation normally relinquishes that power, no matter how friendly its protector might be, except in grave emergencies. Even during the Cold War, Britain and France kept their separate nuclear arsenals, despite our guarantees to protect them.

Fourth, in an effort to "reassure" its trading partners by punishing "malefactors," Washington can make them more anxious. For example, in 1994 the United States put itself on a collision course with North Korea over that nation's nuclear program. Fearful that the North Koreans might be producing a bomb, Washington pushed for economic sanctions and skirted military confrontation. The nations most affected, however—South Korea and Japan—were far more cautious.

They feared that North Korea might collapse, flooding them with refugees, or that, feeling cornered, it might lash out irrationally. We sought to be tough to "reassure" our allies. They warned that we were making the situation worse. When the reassurer rocks the boat, who offers reassurance?

Fifth, playing international gendarme is an expensive proposition that the world's biggest debtor nation can ill afford. It is also a dangerous one. It means that the United States will be perpetually involved in quarrels around the globe in which it has no direct interest, and over causes it will often misunderstand. It was precisely the fear of being dragged into such a conflict, and not being able to emerge without frustration, casualties, and dissension at home, that stayed the hand of the Clinton administration in Bosnia.

The "reassurance" policy so appealing to strategists ignores the fact that our major trading partners have political as well as economic ambitions. They have no objection to being defended by the United States. But they also want the freedom to make decisions and to undertake actions to which the U.S. government might be opposed. They need to be able to act independently of the "friendly superpower," and even in defiance of it.

For this they need strong armed forces of their own not subject to American control. Thus we see that Japan and China are significantly increasing their military capabilities. This is not because they do not trust the United States, but because they want freedom of action to pursue their political goals. Pentagon planners may argue that they are doing others a favor by exercising a friendly hegemony. But in a world of rising regional powers—Japan, China, a German-led Europe, and ultimately a revived Russia—it will not be delegated that authority.

An attempt to police the world, even if intended to be in "everybody's best interests," would have the effect of undermining American interests. Cold War defense budgets have starved our civilian industries of investment funds and increased the power of trade rivals enjoying the benefits of our military umbrella. As they grow relatively stronger, we grow relatively weaker. As illustration, simply consider our relationship with Japan. The end result, as analyst Benjamin C. Schwartz has explained, is that the system we are trying to protect ultimately creates powerful rivals that will weaken our control and replace us—just as we replaced Britain.[7]

The cost of "reassuring" allies does not come cheap. Currently it costs $100 billion a year for Europe, and another $46 billion for Japan and South Korea. Today more than 50 percent of all discretionary federal spending is still devoted to defense, even in the absence of an enemy. While other nations invest for production, the United States borrows for consumption—and in the process becomes ever further indebted to the trade rivals whose interests it determinedly seeks to protect.

For most Americans the defense budget is a mystery, and foreign policy elites would just as soon keep it that way. Patriotic appeals to national defense keep appropriations high. So does the fact that millions of jobs are linked to Pentagon contracts. Despite whatever theories strategists may spin, the defense budget is now, to a large degree, a jobs program. It is also a cash cow that provides billions of dollars for corporations, lobbyists, and special interest groups. Even Bill Clinton, championing "new priorities" during his campaign, pledged to build two weapons systems the Bush administration wanted to cut: the $2.5 billion Seawolf submarine and the tilt-rotor V-22 plane.

All during the Cold War it was considered unpatriotic to question the size of the defense budget. The habit lingers. The public, fearful about jobs and mystified by geopolitical theories, defers to the strategists. The Congress defers to the special interest groups. And the White House, seeking to avoid enemies, defers to everyone.

The defense budget flows from both habit and strategy. To pare it down to size for a world without serious enemies for the United States means to break the habit and confront the strategy. To ask whether we still need to devote so much of our resources to defense is to ask whether the strategy we pursue makes sense in the post-communist, economically competitive world.

The decision has to rest not only on what we can afford. In fact, we can afford a great deal. At times in the past we spent a far bigger chunk of our GNP on defense than today. And we happily throw away tens of billions of dollars for cat food, cologne, and colas. When the nation is in real danger we spend what we must.

But it is not now in danger. Thus the real question is

how much defense we need, and against what. This cannot be answered until we figure out what our interests are. Only then can we determine what kind of foreign policy we ought to have. To do that we have to get rid of a considerable amount of intellectual baggage.

Let us begin with our most important and costly alliance: that with Europe.

4

. . .

Nobody's Europe

Europe as we knew it from 1945 to 1990—the Europe of the superpowers—was the quintessential creation of the Cold War. Divided by armies and ideology, one side was under Soviet occupation, the other dependent on the United States for protection; one side mired in a parody of late nineteenth-century Marxism, the other rushing pell-mell into late twentieth-century consumerism and mass democracy; one side turning deeper inward in an escape from political oppression, the other excitedly declaring its cosmopolitan universalism.

These two Europes assumed strikingly different, and even incompatible, identities. After four decades of Cold War, they hardly recognized each other, and had little in common other than the weight of their troubled history.

At the heart of this divided Europe lay an anomaly. From the ruins of what was once Europe's greatest military and economic power there now rose two states. Neither was quite a nation with a strong sense of identity. Each looked with suspicion and distrust on the other. Both were locked into rival alliances whose very rationale lay in keeping them separate.

Where there was once Germany, there were now "our" Germans and "their" Germans. In the east was a drab and compliant satellite of Moscow, suspicious of the Russians, yet dependent on them for survival. In the west was a prosperous, but politically mute, entity which looked to Washington for its defense, and to Paris and Brussels for its acceptance into the democratic European community.

This divided Germany was both a consequence and a symbol of the division of Europe—just as Germany itself had been the cause of the war that left it, and the rest of Europe, divided. Without Germany's aggression there never would have been a Soviet army in Eastern Europe, or an Iron Curtain. It was both ironical and appropriate that Germany, which tried to submit all Europe to its will, should itself be divided by the power to the east that it had sought to conquer.

If, as was often enough said, this split was somehow unnatural, it also provided certain advantages for most Europeans, and even for many Germans. It meant that Germany at last was a state of manageable proportions. Roughly the same size as France, Britain, and Italy, the new nation of West Germany was not big enough to dominate Europe. Finally, three-quarters of a century after most of the Germanic peoples had been forcibly brought together into a single state, a place had been found for Germany in which it did not pose a threat to its neighbors.

From the division of Germany came the great construction of postwar Europe: the Common Market, and ultimately the European Union. It is highly unlikely that this would ever have been achieved without the division of Germany and of Europe—which is to say, without the Cold War. Nor could it have come about without the encouragement and support of the United States, and without the protection that the Atlantic alliance provided. America was both the progenitor of Western Europe and its midwife.

The Cold War saved Europe from itself. Nations that had proved twice in this century to be incapable of living together in harmony, or even in mutual toleration, were forced to do so by their dependency on their guardians. In dependency and division Europe—or at least the greater part of it that lay in the West—found tranquillity, democracy, and prosperity. For this Europeans have the United States to thank, however much they have complained about American "hegemony."

Toward Europe ours was a beneficent hegemony, exercised with a relatively light hand. In crucial matters of defense and diplomacy, and sometimes in economics, the European allies found it prudent to defer to Washington. Although they had little fear of unprovoked Soviet aggression, the American military guarantee was reassuring, and it spared them the full cost and inconvenience of providing for their own defense.

If the Cold War tranquilized Europe, it energized the United States. It provided Americans with an adversary that was threatening and alien, and with a role as protector of nations that had once been equals. This was a burden, but it was also flattering. The child of Europe had become the successor to Europe.

Although we sometimes chided the Europeans, once they became rich and self-indulgent, for not paying the full price of their defense, there was little bite in our complaint. Indeed, we rather liked it that way because it meant that they deferred to us on matters of defense and diplomacy.

Thus from the beginning of the Cold War NATO was an arrangement by which the European allies pretended to object to their "domination" from Washington, and the United States pretended to be distressed that the allies were not carrying their fair share of the burden. This served everyone's purposes and should have fooled no one. It was the secret truth about NATO that nobody wanted to admit.

The Cold War, and the division of Europe into two rival alliances, was actually a force for stability. In reducing the size and strength of Germany it removed from Germans the temptations to dominance that have brought them, and other Europeans, such grief in the past. It put American soldiers on the Continent in great numbers, where they reassured Europeans against both the uncertain ambitions of the Red Army and the possible stirrings of a reawakened Germany.

Above all, it kept a restraining hand on the simmering hatreds of unassimilated ethnic groups in Eastern Europe—even though we did not sufficiently appreciate this at the time. Fear of the Soviet Union, and the iron hand of local communist authorities, ensured for nearly half a century a deceptive tranquillity in Eastern Europe. But we are only now beginning to realize how fragile that tranquillity was, and how much it depended on control from the top rather than self-restraint from below.

Finally, the Cold War made the nuclear problem manageable. We lived in a nuclear nightmare, but not in a state of nuclear anarchy. The Russians maintained strict control over their weapons, just as we did over ours.

Today, with the breakup of the Soviet Union, there are nuclear weapons in Ukraine, in Kazakstan, in North Korea, as well as in India and Pakistan, in China, in Israel, and in the hands of black marketeers and an international Mafia that is willing and able to sell them to the highest bidder. What the Soviets once controlled now threatens to become a free market.

We have sought to prevent rogue states from acquiring such weapons. But our ability to do so is sharply limited—and in large part because of the collapse of the Soviet Union. When Moscow was Iraq's protector and major arms supplier, it could restrain Saddam Hussein's nuclear ambitions. The same is true of North Korea. But today these states are controlled by no one—except their own ambitious leaders.

But the greatest consequence of the Soviet collapse, and the loss of superpower control, can be seen in Europe. When the Berlin Wall came down in November 1989, with it went the very structure of Europe. The entire continent suddenly moved east. Berlin, instead of being a frontier outpost of Western Europe, was now at the center of a new Europe that extended to the Russian border.

With the change in geographical frontiers has come an equally profound change in political balance. Russia, and even the United States, are now less important in the new European equation; Germany far more so. Whereas the key decisions over Europe were once made in Moscow and Washington, they are now increasingly being decided in Brussels, and probably eventually in Berlin.

The wall between the two Europes, as between the two Germanies, turned out to be more easily removed physically than psychologically. The countries of Eastern Europe—for decades sullen but relatively tranquil—soon became fearful and disorderly. A familiar, and in many ways tranquilizing, authoritarianism was not so easily rejected.

The discredited communist bureaucrats, now repackaged as nationalists, won popular support with promises to bring stability and prosperity to countries that had neither. And they struck powerful chords of anxiety by raising old ethnic animosities. Eastern Europe had been frozen in a time warp. It reemerged as it had entered, untouched by the decades of democracy and wealth that have so dramatically changed Western Europe. Throughout the entire area the past returned with a vengeance.

Western Europeans, who once passed pious resolutions urging the liberation of their brethren to the east, have been shaken by economic demands and by waves of unwanted immigrants. The cozy little Common Market—which they called their Community, and now more hopefully describe as their Union—is being assaulted by East Europeans who insist on entry into what has been an exclusive club.

The West Europeans are torn between their assimilationist rhetoric and their self-interest: between throwing open the doors and putting up walls. There is no easy answer. To remove all barriers—as the West Germans did when they swallowed communist East Germany in one indigestible gulp—is to threaten social stability at home. Yet putting up barricades is no solution, for unrest spills across frontiers in the form of immigrants from the south and east seeking jobs, and refugees fleeing ethnic wars.

Suddenly Western Europe, so confidently entering the twenty-first century as a prosperous and stable post-industrial society, is now becoming simply Europe, with a host of unresolved economic, demographic, and political problems. At this point it is far from certain how it will meet these challenges. It could become one of the world's great powers, or it could descend into a congeries of bickering nation-states.

Atlanticism—the organizing principle of American postwar policy toward Europe—was built on Europe's military and political dependency. This was the lens through which the United States saw itself in relation to Western Europe, and it inspired a host of institutions and bureaucracies to manage that relationship. NATO, the linchpin of Atlanticism, was the instrument by which the United States, with Europe's consent and assistance, provided for the protection of its allies. It served the interests of both sides so long as Europe's division seemed insurmountable, Soviet intransigence eternal, and European dependency inescapable.

But as these conditions have eroded, so has Atlanticism. With the Soviet Union transformed from an evil empire into an impoverished and confused supplicant, it poses far less of a military threat to Europe. Indeed, for the foreseeable future Russia poses virtually none at all. Less needy of American protection, West Europeans are no longer so accommodating to Washington's economic and political wishes. The hard bargaining over the 1994 GATT accords, when the United States was forced to make significant compromises on trade issues, was a sharp indicator of the new relationship among the Cold War allies.

The passing of the old order signals the resolution of

certain problems—such as a Soviet Union that threatened to impose its will on Western Europe. But it also
unleashes others: some new, some until now repressed
or concealed.

First among these is the emergence of a Europe that
is already a serious economic competitor and is likely
to become a political one. The European Union is now
a larger market than the United States, its industries
as productive, and most of its people at least as well-
educated and prosperous as Americans. In the past we
often used Western Europe's military dependency to
gain economic or political concessions. But the end of
the Cold War removed that lever. Tomorrow's Europe
may speak in one voice or several. Its common language
may be English, but its accent will not be American.

Second, European nationalism is growing, and not
only in the east. Yet it is in the former communist-
controlled states that the problem is the gravest. Although we rightly celebrate the fall of communist dictatorships, the fact remains that most of these states have
been frozen in an authoritarian mold for nearly half a
century. They have been cut off from the forces of democratization and modernization that have transformed
the rest of the continent. In some of them communists
have returned to power under new labels. Others flirt
with forms of right-wing authoritarianism and milita-
rism. Most are plagued by unemployment and social unrest as they try to adjust to the pitiless logic of the market.

The very cohesion of some of these states is threatened by ethnic and regional resentments of the kind so tragically played out in the former Yugoslavia. The most difficult task facing European statesmen will be that of absorbing into a peaceful, prosperous, and democratic Western Europe a part of the continent that has known none of these virtues and may have great difficulty acquiring them.

Third, the end of the Cold War means the emergence of that enduring issue of modern European history: the German Question. The Atlantic alliance came into being not only to reduce temptations to a marauding Russian bear and wrap the Europeans in an open-market trading system. It was also designed to reassure Europeans that the Germans would be restrained by a net of embraces and mutual obligations. For them the presence of a large American army on German soil was reassuring as a brake on German power.

The Germans greatly benefited from the American-Soviet competition. They gained protection from Moscow, U.S. aid to rebuild their economy, reconciliation with their Western neighbors, and sanction for rearmament only a few years after their war of aggression. They also won leverage, on that distant day when the Soviet hold on the eastern German lands loosened, for the unification of Germans under a single flag.

The German Question—how to find a place for a unified Germany in a divided Europe—returned in full force with the sudden collapse of the regime in East Berlin. In the drama and the confusion, the seemingly imposing barriers to German unity tumbled. Soviet security interests, fear on the part of Germany's neighbors, anxieties even in the Federal Republic over the costs and consequences of pell-mell unification—none of this stood in the way. It was not the superpowers meeting at a summit who decided the fate of Germany, but the Germans, who seized an opportunity in Russia's weakness and America's acquiescence.

With a unified Germany we are living in a very different world from that of Cold War Europe. Whereas the Federal Republic looked west to North America and the Common Market, the new Germany also looks east, where it has no serious economic or political competitors. With the two German states now integrated, we are witnessing the emergence of what was once called *Mitteleuropa:* an Eastern Europe dominated economically, politically, and culturally by the powerhouse of Germany. The economies of the Czech Republic, Hungary, and Slovenia are increasingly linked to that of Germany. Poland, Slovakia, Croatia, and Rumania will serve, as Mexico has for the United States, as low-wage workshops for German industry.

In a German-dominated Eastern Europe there would be a special place for Russia. But the old roles would be reversed. In place of a Soviet military colossus there would be the German industrial engine driving the economies to the east. The role of Russia and Ukraine would be to serve as a source of labor, raw materials, agricultural products, and low-skill manufactured goods.

The former superpower is likely to become the economic satellite as Russia and Germany return to a more historic relationship.

Fourth, how will Russia fit into the new Europe? Cold War politics focused exclusively on fears of Russian expansion. The problem now is that Russia's contraction may lead to implosion. The failure of Boris Yeltsin and his Western-looking reformers could bring about spreading anarchy followed by militant fascism. While Russia has been too gravely weakened to pose the military challenge that it did during the Cold War, this would upset the peaceful new European balance and push the emerging European Union in a military direction. It would also impose new burdens on the United States.

During the worst days of the Cold War the American-Soviet relationship was described as that of two scorpions in a bottle, each poised to sting the other in a suicidal spasm. Today, they are more like two dogs on the same chain. The Russians need us to ease their transition into the world marketplace. We need them to play a responsible role in the new European power balance.

It is not in our interest that their government be seized by frenzied nationalists or resentful generals. We need a Russia that will be able to keep internal order, be responsible in the world community, and remain open to pluralism and democracy. We must think about Russia as we did about Germany and Japan after World War II. We helped bring prosperity to those former aggressors to ensure our own. Today a stable global order requires a reasonably strong and prosperous Russia. And this requires significant help from the West.

For the foreseeable future Russia is likely to be a peripheral player in the European equation. It will make its power felt defensively—against what it believes to be threats to its territorial integrity or basic security interests. But it will not be able to pose the kind of threat that it did during the Cold War.

The weakness of Russia, the strength of a unified Germany, and growing nationalism in Eastern Europe have turned the logic of NATO upside down. What started as an alliance to defend West Europeans against Russia has turned into one for protecting Europeans against themselves. NATO planners have redefined the mission of the alliance as one of "peacekeeping" and seek to expand its purview across the troubled lands of the old Soviet empire. Many want to bring in the East European states as members, and to expand its ability to conduct military operations beyond Europe.

The purpose of these enlarged goals is to make NATO "relevant" at a time when its original purpose— blocking Soviet expansion—has disappeared. It is quite understandable that the East European states should want to be brought into an expanded NATO. It enhances their sense of security, whether the danger comes from a revived Russia, aggressive neighbors, or once again a hostile Germany.

But this was not the agreement under which the

United States organized NATO. We did not pledge to come to the aid of any European country embroiled in a quarrel with its neighbors. All we intended was to put the Russians on warning that they had expanded their influence as far west as they would be allowed to go. This goal was accomplished.

If we expand NATO further east, how far are we willing to go? To the border between Poland and Ukraine? To that between Ukraine and Russia, or Moldava and Russia? At what point does an expanded NATO become an anti-Russian alliance, directed against a country with a fledgling democratic government that we want to, and for our own sake must, encourage? Or do we then include Russia in NATO as well? In that case, whom is the alliance directed against? If everyone is under the umbrella, who is outside?

This raises a second problem. What happens when those under the umbrella start squabbling with one another? Europe's borders were cast in cement during the Cold War, but no more. Both Czechoslovakia and Yugoslavia, two creations of the Versailles peace conference, have already broken up. Of the new states, Bosnia, Macedonia, Moldava, Ukraine, and Belarus will all likely see their frontiers redrawn. At what point does NATO become involved? By what terms does it define aggression?

If everyone is supposed to be embraced in a state composed of his ethnic brothers, what about the 25 million Russians living as despised minorities in new countries that were once part of the Soviet Union? What about the 1.6 million Hungarians in Rumania and the 500,000 in Slovakia? Will there not be demands that state borders be redrawn to unite these minorities with their ethnic brethren? Will this not be cited as aggression? Will NATO then be instructed to come to the rescue? And on whose side?

Unstable frontiers are just part of the wider problem that NATO planners never envisaged: that Europe's greatest security problem is now aggression within borders. Ethnic conflict is not limited to the former Yugoslavia and is likely to spread elsewhere. The rights and wrongs of such conflicts will not be easy for Europeans to sort out. We have seen this in the Bosnian war, where Serbia, too, has its allies, and in the bitter feud between Greece and Macedonia.

All this poses a dilemma for American policymakers. They want to retain NATO, which gives the United States a military and political role in Europe, and they do not fully trust the Europeans to handle their own affairs. Yet they also know that transforming NATO into a police force to control unruly Europeans is not a priority that can easily be justified to a skeptical American public.

The inauguration of the "Partnership for Peace," which offers second-tier association to the Eastern European countries and possibly to Russia as well, was designed to ease the pressure for a formal expansion of NATO membership. But it does not solve the problem of America's relationship with such an organization. Are we, as NATO doctrine declares, to treat an attack on any member state as one on the United States itself? Does this include a border war between, for example, Hungary and Slovakia? What about the new states that until recently were part of the Soviet Union, what Russians call the "near abroad"?

The problem with NATO is that changes in world politics have outrun the organization's logic. When we were defending Western Europe against the Soviet Union, the alliance cost more than $100 billion a year. It still costs us nearly as much, even though we can no longer identify an enemy. While there is an argument for keeping certain defense structures intact, they must be more firmly grounded in political reality.

Eventually the United States is going to have to withdraw from its putative role as Europe's peacekeeper. That is not a role that we can afford or that the American taxpayer will support. Our reluctance to become involved in the Yugoslav civil wars is the handwriting on the wall. The United States will defend the Europeans from the Russians or another aggressive hegemon, but not from their ethnic wars with one another.

Trying to maintain an outdated dependency—either from a reluctance to relinquish control, or from a belief that the Europeans are incapable of dealing with their problems—is neither in Europe's interests nor in ours. The Europeans will not behave responsibly until they are obliged to exercise responsibility. They have the means to do so. What Europeans have lacked is the will. And that is because they have had little need to develop it.

During the heyday of Atlanticism, the notion of a self-reliant Europe seemed fanciful. General de Gaulle's vision of a European community stretching "from the Atlantic to the Urals" was denounced as impractical and even anti-American. But today it is both feasible and necessary. And as we confront our growing social and economic problems, we should welcome, rather than petulantly resist, the creation of a responsible Europe that takes care of itself.

This wider entity can be called any number of things: a European Defense Community, a Concert of Europe, even NATO. But whatever the label, our needs and Europe's realities dictate that it must be an alliance among Europeans. The notion that the United States must be responsible for Europe's defense is a relic left over from the Cold War. It is kept alive by those Europeans weaned to the pleasures of dependency, and those Americans unwilling to relinquish the reins of a vanishing authority.

We have interests in Europe, for Europe, and in some cases against Europe. This means that we must act unsentimentally upon our wider interests. It means thinking of Europe not as a dependent, or even any longer as an ally, but as a trading partner, an economic competitor, and in some cases as a rival.

Those who believe that through NATO the United

States can exercise tutelage over Europeans for their own good are doomed to disillusion. Our strategists may think that we alone have the wisdom to pacify Europe, and a carte blanche from Europeans to do so. But this is not the way the world works.

Europe is in process of rapid evolution. On one level it is becoming more open, more democratic, more innovative, more linked in its parts, more aware of a common destiny. On another level it is struggling with demons from the past in the form of nationalism and ethnic and religious intolerance.

In the years ahead Europe will be troubled by a complex of trials that will put its tolerance and political cohesion to the test: trials of nationalism, ethnic conflict, racism, immigration, and economic hardship. We must be hopeful that Europeans will surmount these trials and proceed peacefully toward greater degrees of cooperation.

But the United States is not a European nation, any more than it is an Asian nation. It is an Atlantic power, and a Pacific one, with interests in both continents. During the Cold War, as in the two other European wars of this century, that interest lay in preventing any single nation—and particularly a hostile, totalitarian one—from gaining control of the continent. That remains an American interest; but that is not the problem confronting Europe today.

Europe is no longer the single cradle of American civilization, no longer its most dynamic trading partner, no longer, because of a linked history, its special responsibility. The Cold War engendered a unique kind of alliance, and the end of the Cold War has—along with the profound changes in the world economy and America's own needs—undercut the reasons for its continuance. This is the problem confronting the old vintners who so earnestly keep trying to pour new wine into a cracked bottle.

5
...

Visions of Order

Americans are inveterate optimists. We look on war, and even on conflict, as an aberration. We believe that once "the job is done" and the aggressor defeated, the world will return to its normal state: that is, to peace.

This is what we assumed after each of our major wars of this century. And each time we were disillusioned. After our victory against imperial Germany in 1918 we retreated into isolationism, deciding that European politics was too sordid for us. After our victory in 1945 against Nazi Germany and Japan we turned our own society upside down in a frenzied search for "traitors" who alone, we believed, could explain the betrayal of our dream of universal harmony among nations.

Now, after the collapse of our adversary in 1990 and the discrediting of communism as an ideology, we are once again seeking to grasp the holy grail that will usher in the long-awaited millennium of peace and justice.

George Bush, seeking to invoke this spirit in support of his war for the liberation of Kuwait, called for a "new world order" in which a unified international community would punish aggression.

The United States, he explained, was acting as the leader in such a "new world order where diverse nations are drawn together in common cause to achieve the universal aspirations of mankind—peace and security, freedom, and the rule of law."[1]

Motivated by the need to harness public support for a costly war, Bush deliberately drew on a deep-seated American idealism. Using inspirational Wilsonian phrases, he held out the promise of an international community, under American leadership, uniting to defend democracy and guard the independence of nations. Its instrument would be the friendly armada of what Bush described as the world's "sole superpower."

The quick and overwhelming American victory over Iraq set off a tide of triumphalism. Policymakers and columnists assured us that the United States could now act with impunity wherever it chose. With the Soviet Union gone, we had both the freedom and the moral right to intervene at will against aggressors. This was our "unipolar moment."

It was not long, however, before it became clear that the Gulf war was less of a turning point than it seemed at the time. The Emir and his retainers returned to Kuwait, as did Saddam Hussein to Baghdad. The Saudi throne is no less vulnerable than before. We are as dependent on foreign oil as ever. And the Gulf states, North Africa and the Middle East, and even Central Asia remain inviting targets for Iranian-style fundamentalist movements.

The belief that the Gulf war would usher in a "new world order" rested on certain assumptions. Among these are:

(1) that future disturbances of the peace could so easily be categorized between right and wrong, and that future disturbers would be such obvious villains as Saddam Hussein;

(2) that America's trading partners would not only pay for this expensive operation, which ultimately cost more than $150 billion, but for future ones as well;

(3) that future victories against regional tyrants would be equally quick, and equally cheap in American lives, and thus equally supported by the American people;

(4) that an international alliance, and public support, could be assembled in future cases where a vital commodity—in this case oil—was not involved;

(5) that in the future the United Nations would so readily endorse an essentially unilateral American military action.

All of these assumptions pose problems.

First, most aggressions are not so blatant as Iraq's, and most important regional powers are able to rally support from other states.

Second, our trading partners will follow our lead, and pay for our actions, only when it is in their interest to do so. The Japanese and Germans, who under pressure contributed billions of dollars to this operation, made it clear that they would never be so dragooned again.

Third, the Iraqi war lent itself to the kind of knockout force the United States is best equipped to deliver. Against highly motivated and entrenched guerrilla armies the story would likely be different, which is why the Pentagon so vehemently resisted being drawn into the Bosnian war.

Moreover, this war was special because it involved oil, a product about which the industrialized world cares deeply. And it was a concern for cheap oil, not the indignities heaped on Kuwait's royal family, that induced Congress to support the war. Bill Clinton learned about the difference between economic interest and sentiment when he flirted with the idea of intervening in Bosnia.

Finally, the U.N. endorsed the American intervention not because most of its member nations abhor tyrants or are shocked by aggression but because it was in their self-interest to do so. And the Russians, who previously served as Iraq's patron, withheld their power of veto because they did not want to alienate the Western nations supplying them with sorely needed economic aid.

Particularly problematic for the future are assumptions relating to the United Nations and the enhancement of its "peacekeeping" and "peacemaking" powers. Not long ago the U.N. was scorned, not least of all by U.S. government officials, as meddlesome and irrelevant. The end of the Cold War has given it a new lease on life.

With the American people less willing to support unilateral military interventions, the U.N. serves as a useful alternative. Indeed, it has become the vehicle for actions that member nations are unwilling to take without international cover, or for which they do not want to be held fully responsible.

During the Cold War the U.N. was not much more than a debating forum. The big nations lectured one another, while the small ones, persuaded by bribes or arm-twisting, lined up dutifully with their votes. Various Third World dictatorships would support one another in the name of anticolonialism, and, while defending international terrorism, would ritualistically denounce such presumed threats to the peace as "Zionist imperialism."

Although the U.N. has vastly expanded its ambitions, its structure remains unchanged. It is not one that inspires great confidence. A large number of its member states are led by authoritarians more interested in monopolizing power than in spreading democracy. The majority of members neither pay for U.N. military actions undertaken in their name, nor do they assume responsibility for them.

The U.N. was not designed to be a world government, nor the collective conscience of mankind. Rather, it is a marketplace where deals are struck and interests protected. In this it is more like a city council than a forum of wise men. Those with power, or wealth, or other suitable inducements can usually determine how a vote will turn out.

Like any organization, it is based on certain rules. Primary among these is the sanctity of international frontiers. It was easy to assemble a majority against Saddam Hussein not because he was evil, nor because he persecuted Kurds, Shiites, and democrats within Iraq, but because he invaded another state. If there is one principle to which all states are deeply dedicated, it is the inviolability of their own borders.

It is a truth, however regrettable, that great powers have traditionally been bound by those decisions they choose to be bound by, or which other great powers have been able to impose upon them. As illustration one has only to consider the recent record of the United States before the World Court. When the communist-inspired Sandinistas ruled Nicaragua, they brought suit against the U.S. government for sponsoring a clandestine war against them, including acts of sabotage and aid to the Contra rebels.

In due course the Court ruled in Nicaragua's favor. The Reagan administration then denounced the Court as biased (even though a few years earlier the Court had unanimously endorsed a U.S. complaint against Iran for seizing our embassy in Tehran and holding hostages) and refused to abide by its decision. No one proposed a resolution to force the United States to comply. Such are the privileges of the strong.

Our support of the U.N. rises and falls in direct proportion to the degree to which it behaves in ways that our officials find either helpful or troublesome. Approval of the organization was at its height during the Gulf war because the U.N. acted, in effect, on instructions from the White House. We deputized the Security Council, which in turn provided multilateral cover for what was essentially a unilateral U.S. military action with some allied support.

But when a vital interest (like oil) is not involved, when military operations go awry, when "surgical strikes" become carpet bombing, and a promised quick victory degenerates into a costly standoff, support evaporates. Thus, President Clinton, having originally supported the U.N. relief operation in Somalia, backpedaled fast when Americans started to get killed. From the podium at U.N. headquarters in New York he declared that "if the American people are to say 'yes' to U.N. peacekeeping, the United Nations must know when to say 'no.' "[2] He apparently forgot that he could say no simply by casting a U.S. veto in the Security Council.

All nations have tried to get the U.N. to do what they cannot do, or do not want to be seen doing, themselves. This creates a serious problem. There is no international consensus on the rules of a post–Cold War world, or on how to provide the military means to enforce them. Yet no single nation, not even the "sole superpower," has the authority or is willing to pay the costs of trying to resolve international disputes unilaterally.

The Gulf war, with its hopes for a U.S.-led and U.N.-enforced "new world order," is not turning out to be a likely model for the future. An international society is still more an aspiration than a reality.

The United Nations was set up to deal with a world of states in potential conflict with one another. That is still what it is best organized to do. As we have now learned, it was the artificial stability of the Cold War that fortified the power, and the pretensions, of the nation-state. As the world economic system becomes ever more sophisticated, the political system reverts to more primitive forms.

The change in global politics from war between states to war within states can be seen in the civil conflicts in Bosnia, Cambodia, Somalia, and Rwanda. U.N. operations in these countries cost more than $3 billion a year. Yet even with these efforts, the U.N. is barely able to keep up with, let alone control, an epidemic of tribal conflicts, ethnic struggles, systemic breakdowns, and wars of all against all.

Whether from such wars, or from a global economic system that neither knows nor respects national frontiers, the very structure of the modern state system is being eroded. There is today a profound disjunction between our political rhetoric, with its utopian notions of "world order," and the disturbing reality of a world splintering into ethnic and regional parts. It would be foolhardy to predict which states twenty years from now will retain their current borders, or which ones will be spared civil conflict. It would be far more foolhardy for the United States to declare that it will not tolerate such changes or such conflict.

Policymakers in the industrialized states live in a world of integrated economies, global markets, and interchangeable currencies. For them, borders and ethnic groupings are irrelevant, or at best a troublesome distraction. For many of those living in this multinational universe, the notion of loyalty, on anything but a personal level, seems outdated and even anachronistic. Universalist themes and grand global conceptions guide them.

Yet outside the sleek office towers of the multinationals, much of the planet is moving in a different direction. Fear of "the other" and the struggle for survival govern those on the streets. During the Cold War the ominous metaphor for the future was Orwell's totalitarian *1984*. Today it is the corporate police state of *Blade Runner,* or the Hobbesian jungle of *The Road Warrior.*

Allusions to a "new world order," like so much of American foreign policy idealism, is rooted in the rhetoric of Woodrow Wilson. The most ardent of our visionaries, he led the United States into the European war in 1917 with the announced goal of nothing less than "to make the world at last free."

Wilson had not only a vision, but a plan. One part of that plan rested on his belief that aggression by rogue states could be blunted, or even prevented, if all nations—joined together in an international organization—agreed in advance to confront and repel the aggressive state. This was called *collective security*. It was the inspiration for both the League of Nations and its successor, the United Nations.

He also believed that ethnic or religious groups living as minorities had the right to form independent states of their own. Such a policy, he assumed, would reduce international strife. This was called *self-determination*.

These Wilsonian principles of collective security and self-determination were invoked after each of the great wars of this century: World War I, World War II, and the Cold War. Wilson drew up plans for the League in 1919. But he was unable to persuade the Senate to agree to American participation on his terms. The League failed to restrain German, Italian, and Japanese aggression in the 1930s. Although the United States helped organize the United Nations after World War II, that body was mostly irrelevant to the undeclared war between the United States and the Soviet Union.

Once again these principles are being evoked as building blocks of a "new world order." Political leaders everywhere pay allegiance to them. People fight and die in their name. But in practice there is sharp disagreement about what they mean and how they should be applied. A quest for liberation is, in another light, an act of secession. Collective action can represent either the conscience, or the tyranny, of the majority.

Let us take, first, the concept of collective security. It calls for nations to band together to punish aggressors under the authority of a wider military organization, such as NATO, or a wider political one, such as the United Nations. Presumably the member nations would easily agree on who was the aggressor and who the victim in any dispute. They would then dispense justice, and punishment, accordingly. Warlike nations, knowing that they would face a militant world community, would ostensibly refrain from aggression.

Currently in vogue after being long in disrepute as utopian, this is a policy well suited to the present situation of the United States. It can permit a great power to set the agenda and deputize others in the effort. With its declared links to universal democracy and self-determination, it is deeply rooted in the American political tradition. However, even tyrants can subscribe to it when it suits their goals. This is because its guiding principle is the integrity of borders.

Even on its own terms, there are a number of problems with this doctrine. It declares that any act of aggression anywhere is a threat to the peace everywhere. Indeed, it assumes that there is such a thing as "world peace." This is the kind of loose rhetorical language that backfired against Woodrow Wilson.

This is also the language of Harry Truman, another war president. In proposing a U.S. program to defeat communist rebels in Greece in 1947 he declared that "totalitarian regimes imposed upon free peoples, by direct or indirect aggression, undermine the foundations of international peace and hence the security of the United States." This notion of international peace as a natural state, and the assertion that American security depends on it, was on its face absurd, but useful in persuading Congress to back his policy of economic and military aid.

He extended this a few years later when, in defense of the war in Korea, he asserted that "if history has taught us anything it is that aggression anywhere in the world is a threat to peace everywhere in the world."[3]

In truth, what history has taught us is precisely the opposite. Peace is, and always has been, divisible. Iraq fights with Iran but not with Turkey, Serbia with Croatia but not with Bulgaria, Koreans with each other but not with China. Most wars rest on specific quarrels. Otherwise every border squabble, however remote, would trigger a world war.

The danger with such a bloated universalist notion is that it obscures the way the world really works. It describes all disputes as those between good and evil, and turns them into crusades for the soul of mankind. Quarrels between states are always defended on moral grounds, but usually have more mundane origins. By invoking moral arguments, such a doctrine makes possible the use of the most immoral practices.

If one's enemy is absolutely evil (as he usually is, by definition), then any means used against him becomes moral. If all aggression is a crime against humanity, there is little room for compromise. Yet few crimes are so absolute. Every aggressor is not Hitler, every war is not World War II.

Rather than reducing recourse to war, collective security can make it more likely. It does this by elevating local quarrels to the level of regional, or even global ones. This is logically inevitable if aggression anywhere really does threaten peace everywhere. It becomes a self-fulfilling prophecy. Yet a military action conducted by a coalition of strong states against an isolated weak one does not become moral simply because it is unanimous. Morality is not normally defined by numerical majorities.

The virtue of collective security for powerful states is that it is extremely difficult to invoke against them. The major ones have vetoes in the Security Council. Yet it is against such states that collective action is most needed. It is hardly necessary to summon the might of all the world's industrial powers to punish countries like Somalia and Serbia.

By demanding military action against aggressors as a matter of principle, the doctrine of collective security could embroil us in wars everywhere. Invoking this principle, the United States has been recently engaged in, or threatened, military action on three continents: in Somalia, in Serbia, in Haiti. In the first we feuded with warlords, in the second we took sides in a civil war, in the third we declared a ruling regime to be offensive to us.

In not one of these cases could it be argued that a vital American interest was involved. The Cold War, for all its irrationalities, was based on real military, economic, and political issues. With the Cold War behind us, we now engage in conflict for reasons of virtue. However desirable this standard may be for individuals, it is not suited to nations. It can lead either to unending wars for peace in the name of morality, or to a reputation for hypocrisy and empty rhetoric.

In the words of David C. Hendrickson, who has written so incisively on this subject: "What sets the present age apart from the past is, if anything, the belief that the twin ideals of a *Pax Universalis* and a world governed by liberal democratic regimes represent historic possibilities whose absence is a standing reproach to us. Wishing for something that never was, we appear fated to be disappointed by the gap between an idyllic vision and a depressing reality."[4]

■ ■ ■

The other Wilsonian concept—self-determination—is equally potent and equally troublesome. Wilson used it in 1919 to break up the Austro-Hungarian empire and to create a host of new nation-states from it and the remains of the Turkish Sultan's European holdings.

The theory was that every ethnic group should have its own state, and that once this happened, the causes for war would be reduced. The problem was that ethnic groups were mixed up. They did not fit neatly into borders, and particularly not into natural or defensible ones.

States that made ethnic sense made geographic nonsense, and vice versa. Statesmen compromised. The result was a collection of states in Eastern Europe with large, and often resentful, minority groups: Germans living in Poland and Czechoslovakia, Hungarians in Rumania, Rumanians in Russia. This provided fodder for the chaos of the 1920s and 1930s in Europe, and for the infectious disorder now sweeping the states that were kept deceptively calm under communism.

The notion that every nationality and ethnic group should have its own independent territory sounds sensible to most people. But how do you define a people? By race? Language? Religion? Ethnic allegiance? What happens if people cannot be neatly classified?

What if a "people," however we define it, sits on territory claimed with equal fervor by another "people"? Who is right? Serbs or Croats? Jews or Arabs? Armenians or Azeris? Kurds or Turks? This is the problem Wilson faced in 1919 and—by urging the creation of ethnic-based states—solved by pretending it did not exist. This is the dilemma that has caused the tragedy of Bosnia.

In a declared effort to regain their "identities," East European states are now busily suppressing "foreign" ethnic groups in their midst, in the name of self-determination. The result is that the future of Eastern Europe threatens to become distressingly like its past.

If self-determination has been flawed in practice, it is also questionable in principle. It can trigger the disintegration of existing communities and arouse the most atavistic passions. Its central premise is that peoples of different faiths and ethnicities cannot live together in harmony.

This is a principle based on tribal loyalties, suppression of cultural differences, and often intolerance. It encourages prejudice and is prone to violence. This principle has been used to promote the destruction of existing states—as Hitler did in 1938 in demanding the cession of the ethnically German Sudetenland from Czechoslovakia, or as did the Croatians and Bosnian Muslims in breaking up Yugoslavia. It was used to justify the partition of India in 1947, just as it is cited today by advocates of further partition. Currently it is being evoked in an effort to dismantle such advanced industrial states as Canada, Belgium, and Italy.

Such a principle is frequently not only troublesome but destructive. Applied indiscriminately, it is a license to intervention and aggression. It invites majorities to be intransigent, furnishes pretexts for repression, and leads to the atomization of human societies.

It is also contrary, and deeply hostile to, our own experience as Americans—people who have come, and continue to come, from every conceivable ethnic and national group, and who have created a nation far more tolerant of such differences than is any other.

The post–1945 industrialized world was built not on ethnic but on civic nationalism. The United Nations, the Cold War alliances, the global trading system all rested on civic rather than ethnic identities. The Cold War itself ignored ethnic considerations. It was a quarrel of states with an ideological overlay.

The West looked at the Soviet Union and saw both a state and an ideology. The Russians looked around them and saw a multinational empire only shabbily papered over by a half-discredited political faith. When the center cracked in 1990, the world's largest multi-national state splintered into its component parts.

In an effort to maintain power the leaders of a number

of the new ethnically based states have resurrected age-old conflicts with their neighbors and magnified min-uscule differences largely invisible to outsiders. Thus we see the cruel and relentless wars of Armenians against Azeris, of Abkazians against Georgians, and of Croats, Serbs, and Bosnians against one another. Wilson's as-sumption that the self-determination of states leads to greater stability in the international arena has clearly been found wanting. The tragic sequences of events since 1989 in Europe, in Africa, and in the Indian sub-continent demonstrate the reverse.

We can no longer take the principle of self-determi-nation as an unqualified good. The disintegration of states can have a disastrous effect on international sta-bility and on human rights. There can be no automatic right to self-determination when the almost inevitable result—as in the case of the secessions of Croatia and Bosnia—is the suppression of minority rights and a de-scent into ethnic warfare.

If similar catastrophes are to be avoided in the future, we must take a more restricted view of the ideal of self-determination. Otherwise we must intervene with force, or be willing to stand by as states disintegrate in violent conflicts. Unless states are broken up voluntarily, as in the case of Czechoslovakia and the Soviet Union, there should be no presumption of international recognition.

What appeared in 1919 to be a forward-looking principle looks increasingly like a reactionary one. If we believe in the equality of citizens and the protection of minorities, the exaltation of the principle of self-determination (at least in its ethnic form) can be subversive of these ends.[5]

■ ■ ■

At the end of World War II the American public had come to believe that the system of nation-states had been largely responsible for the terrible wars of the century. Only through internationalism and the scuttling of the old diplomatic apparatus, many felt, would it be possible for peoples to live together in peace.

President Roosevelt spoke of a postwar world free of power politics when he addressed Congress after returning from the Yalta conference in February 1945.

> It ought to spell the end of the system of unilateral action, the exclusive alliances, the spheres of influence, the balances of power, and all the other expedients that have been tried for centuries—and have always failed. We propose to substitute for all these a universal organization in which all peace-loving nations will finally have a chance to join.

At the time this seemed not so much an idealistic as a forward-looking statement. The Nazi and Japanese war machines, and the Stalinist gulags, had furnished ample evidence of the evils of the all-powerful state. To many, the state seemed to be the antithesis to the individual and his most formidable foe. Orwell's *1984* captured this feeling with indelible force. And it was not surprising that Kafka's *The Castle* should find receptive new audiences.

But there are states and there are states. In some cases the state can be a prison. Yet under proper controls it can also be the guarantor of individual rights. Constitutional democracy is the instrument by which freedom can be found within the state. In multinational states, ethnic minorities, or religious or social ones, can find protection only under a constitutionally restrained state authority. Otherwise they are the victims of minority fears and majority tyrannies.

Ethnic states exalt group rights. In so doing they leave little room for individual rights. There is perhaps no greater tyranny than that demanded by the ethnic state dominated by its quest for unity and conformity.

If current developments are any indication of the future, we may be reaching an end of the era of the cohesive nation-state embodying diverse ethnic groups. Yet in parts of the world such states, including our own, have been the building blocks of the international system. Without them, the system as we know it falls apart.

How can order, let alone tolerance, be guarded in a world where ethnic and tribal loyalties are becoming ever more important? This is an issue we never thought to address during the long decades of the Cold War when we insisted that it was enough simply to be "free." Now we are learning that it is not enough.

How the constitutional democracies—particularly a bifurcating multicultural one like our own—will protect themselves in such a world has now become for them the most pressing question raised by the collapse of the Cold War order.

6

▪ ▪ ▪

Shibboleths

I t is hardly surprising that Wilsonian idealism should have replaced anticommunism as the guiding light of American foreign policy. With its vision of converting the world to democracy, free trade, and constitutionalism it is deeply ingrained in the bedrock of American exceptionalism. It has inspired both great ambitions, such as our various efforts to "build" nations and implant representative government, and to frequent disappointment when others somehow refuse to learn.

Numerous times in this century we have invaded neighboring countries. We have done this, in Woodrow Wilson's celebrated phrase, to teach them "to elect good men," or because they were excessively disorderly and posed "a public nuisance at our doorstep," to use the official explanation of our 1915 occupation of Haiti. We have intervened, either directly or indirectly, to get rid of governments, usually on the left, of which we disapproved, as in Guatemala, Nicaragua, Cuba, and Grenada. It would be naive to ignore that behind the noble rhetoric about democracy we have often been concerned about the safety of American investments.

And of course we have intervened for humanitarian reasons. Congress and the public have shown an increasing skepticism toward all interventions, even humanitarian ones, that cannot be justified as serving the national interest. The United States remained aloof in 1994 as a reported half-million people were slaughtered in political warfare in Rwanda. France alone, among all the world's powers, sent forces to stop the bloodshed. Nor did the American public support President Clinton's planned invasion to restore an elected leader to power in Haiti (before a diplomatic compromise was reached), despite his appeal on democratic, humanitarian, and national interest grounds.

That hunger in Somalia, tribal violence in Rwanda, ethnic conflict in the Balkans, and repression in Haiti are considered to be our most pressing foreign policy problems is indicative of how far we have left the Cold War behind us. We would probably not be involved in any of these areas—except for Haiti, because of the refugee problem—were it not for the power of television to bring the most horrifying images into the American living room.

The public, distressed by what it sees and accustomed to a host of Cold War interventions in even more unlikely places than any of the above, feels that the government ought to "do something"—but ideally not too much. If the cost rises unexpectedly high, as it did for Reagan in Lebanon and Clinton in Somalia, then the president will have to do an about-face.

Obliging others to elect good men, to discipline disorderly neighbors, to provide relief for victims of disasters, or even to protect investments is an understandable, and in some cases a praiseworthy, action. But such actions are sporadic and limited. And they do not form the basis for a foreign policy.

For this we must look elsewhere: to three lodestars that are often cited as the inspiration for our foreign policy. Each is ritualistically honored and considered virtually sacrosanct. Yet each also involves pitfalls that should not be ignored.

The first of these is *stability*. Everyone extols stability, at least those who are generally satisfied with their situation. This is a rich man's doctrine. It is what guardians of the status quo view as an unqualified virtue. It allows them to maintain what they have in a system that works for them. Stability usually refers to politics and power. But it is generally rooted in economics and the distribution of wealth.

But stability is not a normal state. It has to be imposed, either by strictly enforced rules or a club-wielding power. Since we live in a world without agreed-upon rules, this means that either we learn to live with instability, or that some nation sets itself up as enforcer.

Perpetually in danger of breaking down, stability rests

on power and the will to use it. That also means a willingness to pay a price in blood and treasure. The Soviets imposed stability on Eastern Europe for more than forty years. Eventually that effort, and the arms race, bankrupted them.

The United States is unlikely to find that it is cheaper or easier to stabilize the entire world. During the Cold War we had only an industrially backward Soviet Union as competitor. From this point on we will have to contend with countries like Japan, China, and a unifying Europe, each of which has its own ideas of what stability means and whose interests it favors.

A further problem lies in the weakening of the state system resulting from the collapse of the Soviet empire and the end of the Cold War. That system can impose a form of stability, at least within state frontiers. But as that system has been shaken, there has been a reduction of restraints on group violence within states and on international terrorism. Strong states can almost overnight collapse into weak ones—as the Soviet Union demonstrated—unless their governments are rooted in the allegiance of their people. This is the problem that today confronts the pro-Western governments of North Africa and the Middle East under the impact of Islamic fundamentalism.

Outsiders who attempt to impose stability on warring factions can expect little satisfaction and even less gratitude. Their intervention often produces results counter to their intentions. The British have been trying to impose their idea of order on Northern Ireland for three centuries. In 1915 the United States invaded Haiti to restore stability and stayed nineteen years. The United Nations went to Cyprus thirty years ago to separate feuding Greeks and Turks; its forces are still there.

Since the end of the Cold War we have tried to engage the U.N. in operations that we either do not want to pay for ourselves, such as the Gulf war, or that have little public support at home, such as military intervention in Bosnia and Haiti. The United Nations cannot be a substitute for American diplomacy, and a U.N. army cannot carry out military operations on its own authority. Nor should it, unless we move much further along the road to world government than now seems feasible.

Yet as both Bush and Clinton demonstrated, the utilization of the U.N., and some form of military multilateralism, is often necessary to achieve foreign policy goals. Bush used the U.N. to sanction his attack on Iraq, just as Clinton did to buttress his pressures on Haiti. Multilateralism may be a fig leaf, but it is one that the great powers are likely to rely on increasingly as they incorporate the U.N. into their diplomatic arsenal.

Wars by large nations against small ones do not become just merely because they are conducted in the name of stability. Nor will they necessarily gain the approval of the American people because they have been sanctioned by transient majorities in the United Nations. Our own experience of conducting wars in the

Third World, either ourselves or by proxies, for ostensibly noble causes should induce some modesty when tempted to pursue similar operations in the future.

In addition to a commitment to stability, our foreign policy is concerned with exerting global *leadership*. Few are immune to its heady temptations, even those who preach the need for change and "new thinking." "We are, after all, the world's only superpower," Bill Clinton proclaimed from the White House. "We do have to lead the world." Then, in a less rhetorical mode, he later added that "it's self-evident that we . . . can't solve all the problems."[1]

For half a century, policymakers argue, the United States has been the global leader. Skeptics who warn that we may be overextending ourselves by trying to police the world are dismissed as "declinists." Such critics are accused of underestimating our ability to resist the fate of earlier empires—which ultimately went broke in similar endeavors.

America is "bound to lead," we are told. The Somali relief operation would never have happened without us. Had it not been for American resolve, Kuwait would be a province of Iraq. U.S. threats persuaded the Serbs to lift the siege of Sarajevo, and Haitian generals to allow an American occupation to "restore democracy."

There is some truth in these examples. But they do not furnish a useful guide to the future. They were all operations where we met no resistance from any other major country. But what happens when U.S. leadership runs into the cement wall of another country's vital interests? We had a glimpse of this during the Bosnian war, when Russia—impoverished and enfeebled though it was—made it clear that it had interests in Serbia. In that case the Russians nonetheless gave us considerable room for maneuver, permitting the U.S. to exert political influence while avoiding military involvement. As this showed, when other nations' interests coincide with ours, we can appear to be the "sole superpower." Otherwise, we are often isolated and incapable of action.

Leadership is fine so long as everyone meekly follows. But such situations are rare, and we cannot assume that there will be many of them in the future. In the brave new world after the Cold War, leadership may consist of situations where we plunge ahead and nobody follows. There are words to describe this, but "leadership" may not be the best one.

"A better world can emerge only as a result of strong and enlightened leadership," writes George Bush's national security adviser. "The U.S. alone can provide that leadership. No other power, no international organization, has the global view, and the reach to touch every corner."[2]

This is an exhilarating vision, one worthy of campaign speeches and congressional resolutions. It is also flattering. It inflates our sense of what we can do in the world, and what the world wants from us. We are seeing increasingly that not every country wants to be led by us—not even those most dependent on our military protection during the Cold War.

What they mostly want is not leadership but support. The Europeans would like a pledge that if they yet again engage in war with one another, we will be there to help them out of it. The Japanese would like us to be both their dependent customer and uncomplaining protector. Assorted clients and protectorates, most of them left over from the Cold War, want us to continue to provide bribes and guarantees.

These are benefits they see in our determination to play the "sole superpower" role. It costs them little, and provides them with considerable advantages. But there are sharp limits to such cooperation. Even in the Gulf war, the Europeans and Japanese—whose oil supplies we were protecting—made it clear that this was the last U.S. war they were going to finance.

Leadership has to be viewed as a strategy of foreign policy, not as an objective. It cannot tell us where to go, but only how to get others to help us do what we believe must be done. As a goal it is as seductive, and as deceptive, for a nation as it is for a person.

It is particularly appealing to those in charge of orchestrating foreign policy. Through their lenses the nation's domestic arrangements often seem to be an annoying distraction from the heady work of running the world. The long decades of the Cold War have bred three generations of strategists—military, political, and economic—whose focus starts at the water's edge.

In addition to stability and leadership, the third shibboleth that drives our foreign policy is our avowed duty to promote *democracy*. We extol democracy as though we had invented it, and declare it to be the model system for all mankind. Our politicians instruct others to follow our example, and are perplexed if they don't. We even have a government-funded institution, the National Endowment for Democracy, empowered to promote democracy abroad.

Democracy is the core word of our political rhetoric. Only an American president, after all, could proclaim with a straight face, as Woodrow Wilson did in 1917, that he was taking the nation into a war among European imperial powers to "make the world safe for democracy."

Although he failed in his ultimate goal (we had the war, but did not get democracy abroad), the ambition was not discredited. Now, in the wake of the Cold War, politicians are once again sounding the Wilsonian trumpet.

Yet democracy, if it is to be anything more than an empty slogan, involves certain risks. To take root firmly it usually requires relative prosperity, a secure middle class, and decades of practice. When embraced without adequate preparation, it can lead to terrible disillusion and can degenerate into anarchy or authoritarianism.

We have seen this already in parts of the old Soviet empire. Indeed, Russia itself, having plunged precipitously into free markets and free-for-all elections, could descend into anarchy and militarized fascism through public disgust with incompetence, impoverishment, and corruption.

Further, the "people's choice" is likely to bring some unpleasant surprises. In the few places where it has been tried in the Muslim world, it has enhanced the power of anti-Western fundamentalists. In Algeria in 1992 the military annulled a free election that religious fundamentalists won. Our government, and many others, preferring military authoritarianism to Islamic radicalism, applauded this antidemocratic action. Thus does principle bow to interest.

It is hypocritical to declare that democracy is our highest priority. When it threatens the pro-Western leadership of such states as Egypt, Saudi Arabia, and Russia, our enthusiasm is tempered considerably. There democracy takes a back seat to stability.

This apparently is our approach to China as well. We say that we want the government in Beijing to respect human rights and allow dissidents to speak freely. But we do not want this to get in the way of trade relations. And we have no more interest than do China's leaders in the disruption of a regime with which we have such useful economic and political ties.

Our democratic system has served us well and delineates who we are. But others have had a different historical experience and honor other principles. Some see democracy as anarchical, or human rights as an excuse for subversion, or free trade as a lever by which low-cost producers can take over their markets, or by which employers remove factories to low-wage countries.

Democracy is our system. But we pay a price for it

(just as we do for an economic system of enormous income disparities) in the unregulated disorder, violence, and pornography of our society. We preach it to others. But many question its relevance to societies with different priorities, such as those that put order and wealth above the freedom to do and speak as one pleases.

For example, the virtually life-long prime minister of Singapore, Lee Kuan Yew, contrasted what he called the "breakdown of civil society" in the United States with the "freedom [that] can only exist in an ordered state."[3] Singapore could be described as a "soft" authoritarian state where order takes precedence over unlimited free expression, and political dissent is muted in the pursuit of prosperity. Yet it enjoys a high standard of living, citizens walk its streets in safety, and drugs and violent behavior are not tolerated. Most Americans would not want to live in Singapore. But what lessons can we offer such a country?

It is a reality, however unfortunate, that the developing countries most successful in modernizing themselves and raising the living standards of their people have been relatively authoritarian. This seems to be a price of rapid industrial development.

To illustrate the problem, one has only to compare the records of India and China. India is the world's largest democracy, China the largest authoritarian state. India became independent about the same time that the Chinese communists won the civil war. In those days, during the late 1940s, China was one of the poorest countries on earth. India, by contrast, had a functioning middle class, an industrial sector, and a British-inspired tradition of education and law.

Today the child mortality rate in India is triple that of China. The percentage of illiterate adults is double. The growth rate is less than half. The median age at which people die is twenty-seven years younger. It is not hard to guess which country offers the more compelling example for other developing nations.

■ ■ ■

Foreign policy almost by definition is an elite preoccupation. The average person has little time to devote to its infinite calculations, variations, and possibilities. Unless it impinges on his life directly, as in being called to war, he is generally content to leave it to the experts.

This is not necessarily a good idea. Experts, for the most part, tend to be self-appointed. They are people who make a living in the foreign affairs bureaucracy. Many of these are government officials, from the lowly researcher to the Cabinet member. Others spin out scenarios at government-funded or private think tanks, or teach in universities, or opine about foreign affairs in the media.

They often know a great deal about their subject. But as with every specialty, they are particularly attached to it. They tend to elevate it in importance above everything else. Often they have little perspective, and lose track of the concerns of the person in the street. They tend to get contorted in considerations of "credibility," "national prestige," and "influence." They are suckers for abstractions like "leadership" and "stability."

These people comprise what we could call the foreign policy establishment. They form no conspiracy, but like every special interest group, this establishment has its own frame of reference and its own agenda. Its members see things differently from the general public. Occasionally they lose their sense of proportion.

This is what happened during the Vietnam war, and was frankly admitted by a high Pentagon official who told his superior in 1967, as opposition mounted to the ever-higher toll of casualties in a war whose logic few could persuasively explain, that "a feeling is widely and strongly held that the 'Establishment' is out of its mind."[4]

With the passing of the Cold War, foreign policy has to be subjected to more rigorous checks of reality and practicality. Wars have to be explained. Sacrifices must be justified. Goals must have some realistic relationship to needs.

The public can, to be sure, be easily manipulated by political leaders and by the media. It can be persuaded that virtually any given place constitutes a "vital interest"—so long as some kind of threat is involved. Communism served as the ideal threat during the Cold War.

Since then threats have been harder to come by. Only in Kuwait, where oil was involved, has a president been able to rouse the public with a post-communist threat. Bandit clans in Somalia, rampaging Serbs in Bosnia, evil colonels in Haiti, genocidal militias in Rwanda—none of these can be portrayed as a threat in the way that communism was.

For decades the public has been overfed on threats. It saw a threat in communism; it now looks out the window and sees a threat on city streets. It is not overly alarmed by the breakdown of order in the world when it witnesses such a breakdown in its own neighborhood. Its interests are immediate and they are real.

The foreign policy establishment thinks in different, more abstract terms. It is concerned with credibility, perceptions, power, structures, balance, challenges, and prestige. It views the world through the lenses of the state. Without the state it has neither patron nor function.

Policymakers often live in a rarefied community. They are cut off, like corporate executives, from those whose interests they are entrusted to advance. Secure in their status, they carry on their activities removed from public scrutiny, and often from public control.

For most of the Cold War the public accepted with little question the elite's foreign policy priorities. Fear of a Soviet threat cemented the consensus. But now the disappearance of that threat has created a gap of both perception and rhetoric.

For the first time since World War II, with the exception of the worst years of the Vietnam war, those who make foreign policy have had to justify their policies to a skeptical public. In the absence of communism, they have not been notably successful in doing so.

This elite has sought to find a replacement for the Cold War in delineating America's "responsibilities" as nothing less than the quenching of global "disorder." Listen, for example, to a highly placed official at a leading nonpartisan Washington think tank. "Massive breakdowns of the civil order are too dangerous for the entire system," he declared in 1994. "We are very slow to get on to this. But ultimately we won't have a lot of choice. If we want to run a coherent society ourselves, we will have to defend legal order at the far reaches of the globe."[5]

Perhaps this distinguished scholar has not noticed the "massive breakdowns of the civil order" that have taken place a few blocks from his imposing office and turned the nation's capital into Murder City, USA. But this would not be unusual, for a hallmark of our foreign policy elite is that it has been more concerned with trying to "defend legal order at the far reaches of the globe" than where Americans live. This "entire system" it is worried about would appear to be not the American Republic but the global trading system.

For the general public the nation's fifty-year preoccupation with foreign policy was seen largely as an onerous burden necessitated by menacing foes. For foreign policy elites it was, by contrast, simply the assumption of America's global responsibilities.

The gap between these two perceptions was reflected in the 1992 presidential election. There George Bush's expertise in foreign affairs was no longer an advantage, but a handicap. The public was concerned about jobs, crime, and health. It was ready for a reallocation of priorities toward domestic concerns and away from extensive overseas commitments.

The predictable elite reaction is to label this "isolationism." Even Bill Clinton, elected to concentrate on domestic issues but insecure within the foreign policy establishment and forgetful of the priorities he himself laid out, has done so. But this is to misunderstand both its cause and its extent.

The public accepts internationalism, both economic and political. Its concern is to prevent this from overwhelming long-neglected and now critical domestic problems. A governing elite that fails to understand this is irresponsible and risks becoming irrelevant.

The public itself is different than it was at the beginning of the Cold War. It is even different than it was at the time of the Cuban missile crisis, or during the Vietnam war. It is more Latino and Asian, less oriented toward the Atlantic, more directed toward the South and the Pacific. It is also more culturally divided into groups where ethnicity, gender, or even sexual preference determine loyalties and interests.

This has a powerful influence on how Americans look at foreign policy. Increasingly, they see it through domestic lenses. Thus Africa has become important because of the concerns of black Americans, just as Israel is important because of American Jews, and Ireland because of the American Irish. With millions of people from Mexico and Central America now living in the United States, it is obvious that this has become a critical area for American foreign policy—and not merely because of its proximity.

Where there is no powerful interest group, or perception of direct threat, the public takes a parsimonious view of intervention. This was dramatically evidenced in the war over Bosnia. Most of the commentators on the major dailies and the television networks ardently espoused intervention on the side of the Muslims. They argued either on moral grounds, or evoked Cold War–style arguments by portraying the Serbs as latter-day communists.

The public, for its part, considered the Balkan quarrel to be distant, perplexing, and unresolvable by outsiders. President Clinton correctly decided that if he jumped in, the enthusiastic pundits in the bleachers would suddenly disappear once the going got rough.

To be sure, the public is sometimes wrong. Its interests are understandably parochial. But foreign policy elites who fail to take those interests seriously, or who engage in intellectual abstractions, betray the country's interests. Their counsel will, and should be, rejected.

It is a cliché to say that our world is smaller than it used to be, but that is true. The general public can no longer be oblivious to the most distant outbreaks of aggression, tribal warfare, or genocide. The media will not let it. With their power to penetrate into the most remote terrain and bombard the citizens of the industrialized nations with terrible images of human suffering, they affect the foreign policy agenda.

The public can be roused to concern, at least temporarily. But it also has a limited tolerance for sacrifice, as we saw in Somalia, where we did intervene; in Rwanda, where we did not, though the humanitarian case for doing so was powerful; and in Haiti, where the president reluctantly ordered a military intervention largely to avoid looking weak—despite public opposition to the invasion—and at the last minute embraced a political compromise that undercut his own pledges but avoided a dangerous confrontation with Congress and a skeptical public.

The lesson we can draw from this is not that the public is fickle, its interest sporadic, its emotions manipulable—all of which may be true. Rather there is a double-faceted problem. First, it is the power of the media to set the agenda. This was true to some degree before television (remember the *Maine?*), but immensely more so in an age of instant images. Whereas great nations used to intervene in obscure and troublesome lands for profit or advantage, today they do so under pressure from media pundits and a public temporarily roused to concern.

The second part of the problem is that there is no longer any consensus for intervention, now that the

Cold War guidelines are gone. So long as we had the Soviets to worry about, the public would support just about any intervention on the grounds of "national security." But today there is no compelling reason to get involved in the myriad quarrels of the world's contentious peoples other than that we feel sorry for the victims. But when the victims turn out to be ungrateful, or the quarrel too complicated for us to figure out, let alone resolve, our natural inclination is to throw up our hands and go home.

With communism gone down the memory hole, we have lost our yardstick. Foreign policy, which during the Cold War often seemed to be either ideological posturing or a deadly game of tit-for-tat, now looks more like a haphazard set of responses based on not much more than TV images or the number of pot shots a president is willing to take from his critics.

The result is that our foreign policy is buffeted by winds of emotion and twisted by media agendas and pressure groups. It lacks either a geopolitical or an intellectual core. We no longer know what America should do or can do. Without such a compass we shall simply continue to flounder from "crisis" to "crisis," not knowing which is truly crucial and how we are supposed to react.

7

...

What America Can Do

During the Cold War, foreign policy was the nation's highest priority. Almost any sacrifice could be, and often was, justified in its name. But today, with our old enemy tamed and communism repudiated, foreign policy often seems to have become nearly irrelevant. To make a sacrifice in its name is viewed as an intolerable burden. When American troops are put in harm's way—which is a normal occupational hazard for those who choose to enter the armed forces—the public demands, as in Somalia and Haiti, their immediate withdrawal.

When the public is asked its view on foreign commitments, it invariably prefers minimal involvement. An extensive survey conducted in 1993 showed overwhelming support for a domestic over an internationalist agenda.[1]

In this poll, which stretched across professional and interest groups, the general public rejected some of the reigning shibboleths of the foreign policy establishment. It opposed promoting democracy abroad if that risked electing an unfriendly government, or human rights abroad if it were likely to antagonize friendly nations with different traditions. Fewer than one person in ten favored self-determination for ethnic groups if that risked breaking up established states into warring regions, or believed that the United States should be the single global leader.

Clearly there is a chasm between a foreign policy establishment mesmerized by notions of American leadership and "global responsibilities," and an American public concerned with drug trafficking and addiction, jobs, illegal aliens, crime, health costs, and the environment. Not since the early days of the Cold War, when that establishment rallied the public to a policy of global activism under the banner of anticommunism, has there been such a gap between the perceptions of the foreign policy elite and the realities of the world in which most Americans live.

This is true even on foreign economic issues. The average working American does not share the view of the elites, and particularly of most economists, that global free trade and market efficiency should take precedence over such presumably "parochial" local issues as unemployment—or that it makes no difference if Japan and the European Union become richer and more powerful than the United States, so long as global trade increases. The angry debate over the North American Free

Trade Agreement in the fall of 1993 went beyond partisan politics. It illustrated the conflict between those concerned with efficiency and global markets on one hand and those worried about jobs in declining industries on the other.

The domestic agenda is a pressing, and indeed a depressing, one. We suffer from the highest rates of illiteracy, malnutrition, infant mortality, violent crime, homelessness, imprisonment, and poverty in the industrialized world. Our country is hobbled by debt, weakened by fears for personal safety, and increasingly divided between the skilled and the unskilled, the jobholders and the unemployable.

Despite a growing economy, the average worker's wage is less than it was twenty years ago. The gap between rich and poor grows steadily. We fall inexorably behind our trading partners, just as each new generation of Americans trails its parents in income and opportunity.

We put a higher proportion of our people in prison than almost any other country. We murder one another at a rate that astounds the world. Whole sections of our great cities resemble parts of the Third World. As in Latin American countries, an affluent elite hides behind gated walls, alarm systems, and security guards. Outside these walls the growing ranks of the uneducated poor become more violent and more threatening.

We have now created a class of people that has jobs but is nonetheless impoverished. We call these people the working poor. They are untrained in modern technologies, sometimes homeless, and everywhere ignored by the political system. Although we live in an ever more stratified social structure, we are loath to call it by its proper name. Indeed, it is considered unseemly, perhaps unpatriotic, to point out that a class society exists.

We hold our society up as an example to the world, as in many ways it is. But virtually no country in Western Europe has a multigenerational underclass. None is plagued by the gun culture that has ripped apart the fabric of American cities and now has spread even to small towns. No other mass culture so extols violence, and in no other Western nation is the civil society so at hostage to unrestrained, and seemingly unrestrainable, violence. Indeed, violence may be the single greatest division between American and European or Japanese culture, and the major reason why these nations may no longer look to the United States as a model and for leadership.

Our domestic troubles are not in a realm separate from our foreign policy. They are an integral part, even a product, of it. A nation that pretends not only to protect, but inspire, the world with its values and achievements must be able to offer at least as much to its own people as to those it seeks to guard. Yet it is here, even more than in our foreign policy, that we have failed abjectly.

Although domestic and foreign policy were put into separate compartments during the Cold War, they are integrally related. The nation's economic health, social well-being, and political cohesion are also foreign policy issues. The kind of division that has been made between them is entirely artificial. A sick civil society is the mark of a weak nation. Gun control and public investment that trains and educates the underclass, and restores to health American cities, may be the single most important foreign policy initiative that the government can take.

A nation prey to drugs, guns, and violence, increasingly stratified by social class, torn by racial tension, and riven by fears of insecurity will be a weakened player on the world stage. It may also be a threatened democracy—its people disillusioned with traditional political parties, prey to the rantings of talk show demagogues and television evangelists, and sympathetic to vote-seeking messiahs inundating the air waves with promises of deliverance from conventional politics.[2] It is not easy to see what lessons in democracy the United States offers the world when Americans themselves increasingly seem to believe that it fails to work in this country.

For this reason a workable foreign policy must be geared to the needs of American society. It cannot indulge in flights of rhetoric, dedicating itself to the pursuit of vague objectives like "democracy" and "pluralism" in lands inhospitable to these values and of no threat to the United States. The result is to invite the failure of our efforts and the disillusionment of the public asked to support such quixotic goals.

The unreality of current notions of national interest

was dramatized by the president's national security adviser at the time of the American occupation of Haiti in September 1994. The enemies of the United States, he declared in a flourish of rhetoric, include "extreme nationalists and tribalists, terrorists, organized criminals, coup plotters, rogue states and all those who would return newly free societies to the intolerant ways of the past."[3] After thus lining up the United States for a crusade against most of the world, it is not surprising that the Clinton administration, in one area after another, has had to retreat upon discovering that it was standing alone.

Having emerged from decades of foreign policy "crises," the country is in no mood for costly adventures in redeeming the world. Leaders who set such agendas are doomed to failure and will be repudiated. The result may well be to discredit not only their more grandiose projects but even desirable ones, such as cooperation with other major powers to dampen regional conflicts. That is the price paid for a lack of a sense of proportion.

As the Cold War marked the domination of foreign policy, so in this post–Cold War period domestic policy has now become paramount. This is natural and entirely proper. It is what happens after every war, and it marks the restoration of a normal balance. Our foreign policy should flow from our domestic society, from the needs and values of the American people—not the other way around, as during most of the past half-century.

Reflecting its emphasis on economics, the Clinton

administration has declared that the obsolete containment doctrine should be replaced with the "enlargement of the world's free community of market democracies."[4] The assumption behind this is that free markets require free societies, and that democracies rarely go to war against one another. But a simple look at the world, beginning with the fast-growing "tigers" of Southeast Asia, reveals that there is no necessary correlation between market success and democracy. The idea that there must be is at best wishful thinking, and at base a provincial conceit, a delusion rather than a policy.

Many countries—Japan, for example—do not use economic growth primarily to expand domestic consumption, as does the United States. They use it to expand production, penetrate foreign markets, acquire assets abroad, and increase their power. Economic power is the foundation of military power. A richer China, to take one case, may or may not be less authoritarian. But, as its ever-growing military budgets indicate, it will be stronger and more assertive. The notion that Japan should have a military potential commensurate with its economic power is no longer a taboo topic in Tokyo.

Tomorrow's America will not, like Cold War America, be dealing with a world it dominates. It will be part of a complex of market economies, some of which will be democratic and some not—but all of which will be unyielding competitors with their own agendas. The days of deference by allies to American military power are over. Indeed, the days of allies are over. In a world without a single menacing enemy, alliances are deprived of meaning. And in trade wars, unlike military confrontations, there are no allies: only rivals.

Even the centerpiece of our Cold War alliance structure—NATO—is sliding into atrophy in the absence of an enemy. Its major function today is bureaucratic and psychological rather than military. It provides a function for general staffs with no military duties to perform, and the illusion of security against enemies now nonexistent. Gradually NATO is likely to be replaced by an essentially European alliance, a latter-day Concert of Europe, focused on a Franco-German nucleus, in which the American role will be sharply reduced.

This is not a cause for regret but rather satisfaction, for it means that the United States can cease being distracted, even seduced, by tasks that others can best perform for themselves. The ritualistic preservation of outworn structures is an evasion that puffs up our vanity and distracts us from the necessary work of reevaluating our interests.

A new American diplomacy—one that leaves Cold War thinking behind—will pose practical questions. It will ask, first, what responsibilities the nation has to itself and to the welfare of its citizens. For what causes should we use our power to intervene militarily, and what price is worth paying? Do we operate alone, or only in conjunction with others? At what point does a humanitarian act—like feeding the hungry or separating victim from executioner—become a political one, like policing and creating a nation? What is the place of morality in foreign policy?

This last question is particularly difficult for Americans. More than any other people, we believe that our foreign policy should have a moral component. The glue that bound together the anticommunist consensus was in part a moral one. Since the end of the Cold War and the disappearance of any serious security threat, decisions about intervention often involve the issue of morality. What constitutes moral behavior on the part of a nation? When is interference in another country's affairs morally justified? These are not easy questions to answer. Well-meaning people can disagree on the morality of a given situation. The inability of the Clinton administration to forge a consensus on the Bosnian war rightly caused it to retreat from its original impulse to intervene. What seemed like a moral outrage to some was to others merely a Balkan civil feud which outsiders could not resolve.

Under what circumstances should the United States intervene in the internal affairs of other nations? There would seem to be two general justifications: morality and self-interest. Under the category of morality, most Americans would agree that intervention is justified to alleviate extraordinary and severe degrees of human suffering, such as famine, plague, and drought. This is what we did in Somalia before the mission became compromised by grandiose notions of "nation building."

In addition to humanitarian relief in the face of natural disasters, acts of genocide cannot be tolerated by the community of civilized nations. When people are being exterminated because of their ethnicity, race, or social class, outside powers have not only the right but the compulsion to intervene. Ideally they should do this in concert, whether through the United Nations or simply by joint agreement. It was shameful that the United States did not intervene in Rwanda in 1994 to stop the slaughter of half a million Tutsi by the rival Hutu tribe. France alone, to its credit, sent its troops to end the bloodshed. It was no less shameful that in the late 1970s not a single Western nation moved against the Khmer Rouge that killed an estimated two million of their own people in their drive to "purify" Cambodia for communism. Finally, it was neighboring Vietnam that entered the killing fields to stop the genocide.

If armed intervention is justified in Rwanda and Cambodia, why not in Bosnia or in Haiti? Here, as in all political distinctions, the lines cannot be cut with clear precision. But there are major differences that are crucial. Bosnia was the scene of a civil war in which civilians were targeted because of their ethnicity, in which people were displaced from their homes to create "ethnically cleansed" zones, and in which terrible human rights abuses occurred. But this took place in the context of a traditional war over territory, and neither the intention nor the result was the systematic eradication of a people, which is the strict definition of genocide. The United

States has no responsibility to defend break-away states that unilaterally declare their independence.

In Haiti significant human rights abuses have taken place for generations as a ruling elite uses intimidation and terror to enforce its authority over an impoverished proletariat. This is deplorable. But it is also the condition under which much of the world lives. To argue that the United States must intervene to overthrow repressive regimes throughout the world, or even in this hemisphere, is to set an agenda that would lead to perpetual, and ruinous, wars of righteousness. It is a policy that could not be honored, and would be rightly repudiated by the American people.

The lesson of these examples is not that the United States must never intervene for considerations of morality. There are times when it should and must: both in cases where it has the power quickly to stop the horror, as in Rwanda and Cambodia, and in cases where the horror is on such a scale as to undermine the foundations of Western civilization itself, as in the genocidal madness of Nazi Germany.

But if a foreign policy is to be effective, it must have the support of the American public. And to have that support it cannot be quixotic or gaseously utopian. It cannot seek impossible ends, like the democratization of the world, or the attainment of a beneficent "world order." It will avoid grandiose rhetoric precisely so that it can act in those cases—which will be few but critical—where it can at tolerable cost achieve its ends, and where the degree of suffering or injustice that it addresses greatly exceeds the customary or the tolerable. This is not a formula that will satisfy zealots or crusaders, and it is also more than some others may be willing to incur. But it is one that accords with the moral values of the American people and has limitations realistic enough to win their support.

The major justification for the use of force will continue to be, as in the past, self-interest. In a democracy, the interests of the people are, or at least should be, coterminous with those of the state. In practice, as we have seen as recently as the Vietnam war, leaders sometimes have fantastical ideas of the "national interest" and can drive their nation to ruin. In such a case the only remedy is the election of new leaders.

There are a number of occasions when the United States might be driven to use force in the pursuit of self-interest: to protect vital natural resources; to quell regional disorder in areas vital to American security; to defend the nation's borders from, for example, drug traffickers, illegal aliens, and terrorists; to preserve a favorable balance of power in such critical areas as Western Europe; and to prevent nuclear and ecological threats to our national well-being.

Admittedly this is a long list, but it is not an indiscriminate one, and in matters of military intervention, discrimination is all. It does not include interventions to establish democracy, or to make the world a better place, or to combat uncongenial ideologies and religions. It does not set the United States the impossible and self-destructive task of correcting all the world's wrongs or converting all the world's peoples to the blessings of our way of life. It is not a policy subject to spasms of self-intoxication and to crusades of self-righteousness.

The denial of any vital resource to a nation, as an act of hostility or aggression, is traditionally a cause of war. Whether it concerns oil or any other commodity, a great power must defend its interests (although in the case of oil, the United States must also reduce its imports by reforming its wasteful practices).

Where serious political disorder, particularly near our shores, threatens our own stability or that of areas we consider vital to our interests, we cannot, as a great power, abjure the right to intervene. This does not mean that we should, as in the Cold War, behave like a global fire brigade. Rather our interventions, where necessary, should be almost entirely within our own geographic region: North America and the Caribbean.

A nation that cannot control its own borders will have grave difficulty controlling the direction of its national life. While our policies, as an immigrant nation, toward refugees must be liberal and compassionate, they must not be impotent and anarchic. And toward those who mean us harm, like drug dealers and terrorists, we have the duty to protect ourselves with appropriate power.

The notion of the balance of power may have a nineteenth-century ring, but it remains a reality. The United States intervened three times in this century to prevent any single nation from controlling the European continent, and the maintenance of a European balance remains an American interest. The same is true in Asia. If diplomatic means to ensure this fail, force may once again be a necessary recourse.

Finally, and most obviously, threats to our very survival—whether from rogue states or from terrorist groups armed with nuclear weapons, or from states or megalithic corporations that imperil our natural habitat through pollution and the destruction of irreplaceable resources—may in the final analysis be controllable only through the use of force. It is not power that is evil, but only its misapplication.

If force is to be applied, *how* shall it be done? Four possibilities present themselves: the United States can act alone as the world's single most powerful state; it can form alliances with weaker nations, as was done during the Cold War; it can organize temporary coalitions, as was done during the Gulf conflict; or it can try to operate through multilateral organizations such as the United Nations or regional ones like the Organization of American States.

Which device is most appropriate clearly depends on the circumstances. Yet it is clear that with the disappearance of a single serious enemy, formal alliances are of declining relevance and usefulness, kept alive largely through bureaucratic inertia. Temporary coalitions tend to depend on the willingness of a single major nation to organize the action and carry the brunt of the burden, as the United States did during the Gulf war. Multilateral action through the U.N. or other organizations is likely to be invoked increasingly in the future. It takes the sole burden off any single nation and diffuses responsibility. But it is workable only when it accords with the common interests of all the major powers. This usually means reaching the lowest common denominator, as evidenced by the U.N. resolutions on the Bosnian war. And there, of course, the policy was essentially a failure. The U.N. was not equipped to perform the role of an imperial administrator and did not have the support of the major powers to do so.

The current enthusiasm for multilateralism results in large part from the unwillingness of states to make serious sacrifices to establish order in areas remote from their direct concern. The result of this reality is the failure of the organization to act upon its grandiose ambitions, thereby lessening its credibility even in areas where it is capable of action. A further result is to inhibit an alternative approach to crisis-dampening by regional powers with a direct and vital concern in the outcome. The world stood by, for the most part, in Bosnia because the European states vitally concerned were not sufficiently organized to take action, while the United States, which had the power, lacked sufficient interest.

What this anomaly suggests is that regional disturbances that do not threaten the world power balance must be dealt with by the major powers of the region, ideally with the endorsement of the international com-

munity. Rather than seeking an ephemeral global security, we should instead, as Charles William Maynes
has argued, encourage a policy of "regional self-reliance
[that] would recognize that certain powerful states in
each area will inevitably play a special security role."[5] In
other words, we must accept the reality of the long-
standing tradition of spheres of influence—a tradition
that we scrupulously insist upon in the Western hemisphere under our unilaterally imposed Monroe Doctrine.

Such a policy would be more tolerable to those concerned about the equality of all states if other major regional powers were democratic, like the United States
and the European Union, or moving toward democracy,
like Russia. With the Cold War behind us, a benign
spheres-of-influence policy becomes far more feasible
than in the past. It is also more realistic than any alternative.

The recent past should have taught us that regional
powers may be the only ones willing to deal with regional breakdowns. The murderous Idi Amin was de-
posed by neighboring Tanzania, as Maynes has pointed
out, not by the U.N. or the distant great powers. It was
Vietnam that put down the Khmer Rouge's genocide
in Cambodia, and India that stopped the Pakistani army's
extermination campaign in East Bengal. It was the
United States that intervened to restore order in Grenada, Panama, and Haiti, just as Russia alone has either
the interest or the capacity to halt the murderous anarchy

in the Caucasus. It was the blind refusal to recognize the reality of a Chinese sphere of influence that drew the United States into its disastrous war in Vietnam.

A spheres-of-influence policy is the basis of our relationship with Canada, Mexico, and the Caribbean, just as it is for Russia with the former Soviet Union, and China with Southeast Asia. It is how the strong and the weak coexist. It will no doubt seem unjust to those who believe in a global community of equal states, none able to impose any authority over the other. But it is a reality of the world we live in, and it offers a feasible alternative both to indiscriminate globalism and to utopian visions that cannot be translated into action.

Utopianism is just as unrealistic, and as dangerous, as isolationism. We have never truly been an isolationist power, and we certainly cannot be one in a world integrated economically and technologically. But we also cannot afford to indulge in lingering Cold War conceits of military omnipotence and unlimited global responsibilities. Such fantasies are doomed to failure and breed distrust of democratic government.

We have won a victory, of sorts. But that war is over. We enjoy a time of peace, of sorts, although not everywhere, and certainly not forever. Our task now is not so heroic as fighting a war. But it is no less difficult, and in the end it may be as important—that of recognizing our limitations, of rejecting the vanity of trying to remake the world in our image, and of preserving the promise of our own neglected society.

Americans today are hobbled by self-doubt about our own political system and mini-"crises" abroad that in fact pose little danger. Yet in foreign policy the nation enjoys an unparalleled freedom of action. Like Britain at the height of her power in the mid-nineteenth century, we live in a world where we are not unchallenged but are unquestionably first among only potential equals. We have no serious enemies and require no allies. This is our equivalent of what the British called their period of "splendid isolation."

The term has been much abused in recent years. It does not mean that the British were isolated, any more than we are today. Quite the contrary: they were never more engaged in the world. But the engagement was on their terms. "We have no eternal allies and no perpetual enemies," their leading statesman said at that time. "Our interests are eternal, and those interests it is our duty to follow." They lived in a world of other major and aspiring powers that did not always wish them well but learned to respect their strength, their diplomatic agility, and their values.

Ultimately even the most subtle diplomacy could not carry them above the shifting tides of power. But for a century it ensured them security and prosperity. Had they, like the United States, possessed an entire continent of unparalleled riches in a sea of weak neighbors, instead of a beseiged and resource-poor island, their success might have been even greater and more enduring.

As we have left the Cold War behind us, so have we

left the American Century. The war gave us a sense of purpose, and without it we feel trapped by domestic troubles from which we can find no escape in parades, drum rolls, and demonstrations of resolve. The self-confidence that has always been one of our most attractive national characteristics has been sapped, leaving a nation confused and even embittered. For a long time foreign policy was a useful evasion.

It cannot be that anymore. We have to face our domestic problems as the painful compromises that they are. And we must return to foreign policy not as an escape or a salvation, but merely as a means of making our way, without illusions but also without cynicism, in a world of usually competing, sometimes cooperating, states. This is not a heroic task. But it is an important one, for on its success hinges our ability to preserve and enlarge the noble vision that has justly been called the Promise of American Life.

Notes

Introduction

1. Richard M. Nixon, *Beyond Peace* (New York: Random House, 1994), p. 154.

1. An Ambiguous Victory

1. Tony Smith, *America's Mission: The United States and the Worldwide Struggle for Democracy in the 20th Century* (Princeton: Princeton University Press, 1994), p. 348.

2. For the argument pro and con, see *International Security* 17, no. 4 (Spring 1993), with articles by Christopher Layne, Robert Jervis, and Samuel P. Huntington.

2. Interest and Morality

1. George F. Kennan, "The Sources of Soviet Conduct," *Foreign Affairs,* July 1947. Kennan also argued presciently in the same essay that if "anything were ever to occur to disrupt the unity and efficacy of the Party as a political instrument, Soviet Russia might be changed overnight from one of the strongest to one of the weakest and most pitiable of national societies."

2. Ronald Reagan, "Promoting Democracy and Peace," British Parliament, London, June 8, 1982.

3. For an interesting discussion see Daniel Deudney and G. John Ikenberry, "After the Long War," *Foreign Policy* 94 (Spring 1994).

4. Michael Cox, "From the Truman Doctrine to the Second Superpower Detente: The Rise and Fall of the Cold War," *Journal of Peace Research* 27, no. 1 (1990), p. 31. This author also makes a strong argument that the danger that American policymakers saw in Europe after World War II was "not the Red Army, nor indeed the immediate activities of the communist parties, but economic decline. This, it was argued, would in time lead to a radicalization of the communist (and probably the socialist) left—followed by the imposition of greater state control of trade and industry to prevent total economic collapse. A statized Western Europe would then develop closer ties with the emerging planned economies of Eastern Europe. Finally, this developing entity would—it was maintained—forge tight links with the USSR which clearly would have welcomed the reorientation of Europe as a whole away from the world market towards the Soviet sphere of influence. This, in essence, was the meaning of the 'Soviet threat' in 1947" (p. 29).

3. Finding a Role

1. Cheney cited in Robert L. Borosage, "Inventing the Threat," *World Policy Journal* 10, no. 4 (Winter 1993–94), p. 8. Clinton in "Clinton's Words on Somalia," *New York Times,* Oct. 8, 1993.

2. Ronald Robinson and John Gallagher, *Africa and the Victorians* (London: Macmillan, 1961), p. 274.

3. Cited in Borosage, "Inventing the Threat," pp. 7, 9.

4. See Lawrence J. Korb, "Shock Therapy for the Pentagon," *New York Times,* Feb. 15, 1994, p. A19.

5. "Forces and structures . . ." Borosage, "Inventing the Threat," p. 10; Perry in Eric Schmitt, "Lawmakers of Both Parties Challenge 2-War Strategy," *New York Times,* Mar. 10, 1994.

6. Patrick E. Tyler, "U.S. Strategy Plan Calls for Insuring No Rivals Develop," *New York Times,* Mar. 8, 1992.

7. Benjamin C. Schwartz, "The Arcana of Empire," *Salmagundi* 101–

102 (Winter-Spring 1994): "The United States, then," he contends in a provocative study, "is caught in the dilemma that eventually ensnares all hegemons. Stabilizing the international system is a wasting proposition. While other states benefit from the stability the predominant power provides, they have little incentive to pay their 'fair share' of the costs of protection since the hegemon will defend the status quo in its own interests, regardless of what these lesser states contribute . . . Forced to place such importance on 'security,' the hegemon directs capital, creativity and attention from the civilian sector, even as other states, freed from onerous spending for security, add resources to economically productive investments. This leads over time to the erosion of the preponderant power's relative economic strength. As economic, and hence military, capabilities deteriorate, so does the very comparative advantage over other powers upon which hegemony is founded. The hegemon's declining advantage spurs the emergence of great power rivals, requiring the hegemon to spend more on defense to maintain its preponderance, which, of course, only further deteriorates its comparative advantage. And as its relative power declines, the international stability that the hegemon assured is, perforce, unsettled" (p. 203).

5. Visions of Order

1. George Bush, State of the Union address, Jan. 29, 1991, *New York Times,* Jan. 30, 1991, p. A12.

2. Clinton, address to the United Nations, Sept. 27, 1993.

3. Truman (1947) cited in Thomas G. Paterson: *Major Problems in American Foreign Policy,* vol. 2: *Since 1914* (Lexington: D.C. Heath, 1989), p. 298; Truman (1951), p. 408.

4. David C. Hendrickson, "The Ethics of Collective Security," *Ethics and International Affairs* 7 (1993), p. 2. This thoughtful essay was most helpful to me in framing the argument.

5. In this discussion I have benefited from the excellent study by Kamal S. Shehadi, "Ethnic Self-Determination and the Break-up of States," Adelphi Paper 283, Dec. 1993, International Institute for Strategic Studies, London.

6. Shibboleths

1. Clinton: "lead the world," April 1993, quoted in Christopher Layne and Benjamin Schwartz, "American Hegemony—Without a Leader," *Foreign Policy* 92 (Fall 1993); "can't solve," *Washington Post,* Oct. 17, 1993.

2. Brent Scowcroft, "Who Can Harness History? Only the U.S.," *New York Times,* July 2, 1993, p. A15.

3. Fareed Zakaria, "A Conversation with Lee Kuan Yew," *Foreign Affairs* 73, no. 2 (March–April 1994), p. 111.

4. Statement by John McNaughton, assistant secretary of defense, in a memo to Robert McNamara, May 6, 1967, quoted in Marilyn B. Young, *The Vietnam Wars, 1945–1990* (New York: Harper Collins, 1991), p. 206.

5. John Steinbruner, director of foreign policy studies, The Brookings Institution, quoted in Stephen Engleberg, "From the Pall of Sarajevo to the Shores of Who Knows Where," *New York Times,* "The Week in Review," May 1, 1994.

7. What America Can Do

1. *America's Place in the World,* Times Mirror Center for The People and the Press, Nov. 1993.

2. A poll conducted by the Times Mirror Center for the People and the Press in 1994 on voter attitudes toward political issues and parties found an electorate that is "angry, self-absorbed and politically unanchored," one marked by "frustration with the current system and an eager responsiveness to alternative political solutions and appeals." *Los Angeles Times*, p. 1, and *New York Times,* p. A12, Sept. 21, 1994.

3. Anthony Lake, "The Reach of Democracy," *New York Times,* Sept. 23, 1994.

4. Thomas L. Friedman, "U.S. Vision of Foreign Policy Reversed," *New York Times,* Sept. 21, 1993.

5. Charles William Maynes, "A Workable Clinton Doctrine," *Foreign Policy* 93 (Winter 1993–94), p. 10.